T0375107

When it comes to climate change, circularity has become a major topic. Closed loops, reuse, recycling, and renewable materials are fashionable ideas in architecture and product design. In order to establish the new paradigm of circular design, this book introduces an urban and territorial dimension to the goal of transforming living spaces for resilience and sustainability. It proposes to use design-led research and design-thinking for analysis, concepts, strategies, and cooperative processes of transformation. Featuring case studies from all over Europe that relate creative narratives in urbanism to social and economic innovation, *Circular Design* aims to activate dynamic fields and networks of ideas, people, and spaces, oriented to circular principles.

jovis

Circular Design

Towards Regenerative Territories

Jörg Schröder
Riccarda Cappeller
Alissa Diesch
Federica Scaffidi

TABLE OF CONTENTS

8 MESSAGES

10 Circular Design
Jörg Schröder

30 Circular Narratives
Riccarda Cappeller

44 Circular Assets for City and Society
Federica Scaffidi

54 Culture and Creativity as Drivers for Cicular Territories
Alissa Diesch

60 The Atlas as a Project
Alissa Diesch

66 INTERFACE

68 Territorial Relation

70 Context

72 Challenges

74 Situations

76 Scales

78 Strategies

80 Tools

82 NEW SYSTEMS

84 Walk the Line

92 Meat Change

100 Co-Habitat

108 NEW PROCESSES

110 Weserhafen

118 Dinámicas Cafetaleras

126 TRANSFORMATION

128 When Pacman Ate the Motorway…

136 Koshiki Dreams

142 A New Layer for Syracuse

TABLE OF CONTENTS

148 NEW BAUHAUS CITY

150 Rediscovering Territories

152 New Bauhaus City Atlas

154 Superumbau 2035

160 Land Unter

166 SEASIDE

168 Living on the Coast

170 Seaside Atlas

172 Riviera dei Fiori

180 Welcome to Rügen

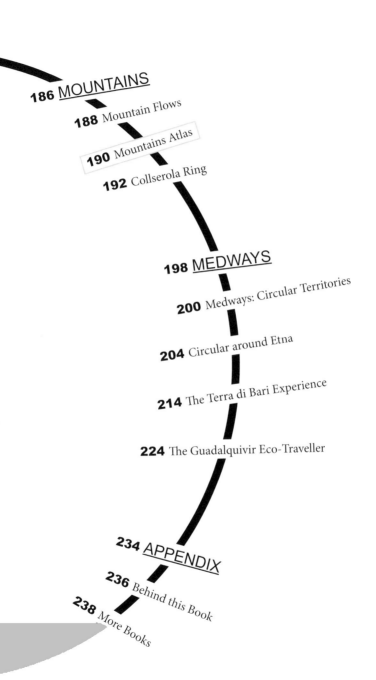

186 MOUNTAINS

188 Mountain Flows

190 Mountains Atlas

192 Collserola Ring

198 MEDWAYS

200 Medways: Circular Territories

204 Circular around Etna

214 The Terra di Bari Experience

224 The Guadalquivir Eco-Traveller

234 APPENDIX

236 Behind this Book

238 More Books

MESSAGES

Circular Design: Design-led Innovation for Circular Territories

Jörg Schröder

Of the total waste generated in Europe, 36% comes from building construction and demolition (Eurostat 2020). A triple challenge for the aim of carbon neutrality is the energy consumed by production and demolition, the use of finite and carbon-based resources, and the energy wasted in transport. Market volatility and rising prices make it an urgent matter to rationalise materials and energy use. The issue of sustainable construction materials—which for the last seventy years seemed an infinite resource—is becoming a driver for change in architecture and in the whole construction economy, with the aim to reduce CO_2 emissions and climate impact (European Commission 2022a). Architectural research and practice is following other creative fields such as fashion, furniture, industrial, and product design to target the re-use of materials not only as a necessity of our time but as a thrilling field of creativity and expression of new aesthetics that strongly influences the economy. The Ellen MacArthur Foundation (2021a) claims that "design is fundamental to a circular economy". Designers promote "circular solutions", establish new circular business models, and see themselves as frontrunners in an "irresistible circular society" (Creative Denmark 2021). It is exiting to detect new links between design disciplines and economics, material, social, and cultural sciences. The design sector—of which architects are a part—is extending the concept of "recycling" to "upcycling" and finally to "designing for reassembly", attempting in the design process to include a further use for the original product.

This essay—and this book—goes one step further to look at the links between circularity principles, design, and city-making, in order to develop a systematic approach. It asks what a circular design paradigm could mean, how precisely it could support climate neutrality, and how it is bound to the sustainability of cities and quality of life. We begin with the topic of waste and resources: would it not be better re-use whole buildings, urban areas, and even cities instead of disassembling them for recycling? Should we take a more comprehensive approach than simply focusing on material recycling, concen-

Architecture and buildings are at the forefront when we discuss how to achieve climate neutrality, how to transform cities and territories, how to achieve inclusion. Here, links between circularity, design, and city-making emerge as one of the most promising generators of innovation. This outline shows that a circular design paradigm needs to start from an urbanistic perspective and why circular design can make cities more liveable.

trating instead on a carbon-free and circular way to design, install, live, and think about space? This essay focuses on the implications of an overall circular approach to city-making, to dealing with urban spaces and urban elements. It highlights the role of design in this process, since circularity in cities is bound to material, spatial, and cultural experience. The objective is to define a combined circular-design approach to the way we analyse, interpret, and project the structure, shape, vitality, and meaning of cities, and the ideas, processes, and mechanisms that shape their transformation. Since design circularity is addressed in different disciplines and diverse scientific, political, and societal discourses with different definitions, roles, and perspectives, the aim of this outline is to contribute to a more systematic understanding of circular design, and to relate it to city-making. Urban design and planning is reaching out to new interdisciplinary linkages, highlighting the conceptual and concrete impact of material culture, visioning, shaping space, and organising processes of change.

This essay looks not only at architecture and urbanism, but also at a wider range of creative disciplines for climate-neutral cities, in dialogue and collaboration with other sectors and society.

Methodology

The focus of the research offered in this essay is on urbanism and architecture, with links to other creative disciplines, to material and natural sciences, engineering, economics, social sciences and humanities. Based on a discussion of decarbonisation and the questions it raises for the role of cities, city-making, and liveability, the essay offers an outline that reviews current concepts and research on circularity, design, and city-making, in order to identify and condense the main characteristics for a circular design paradigm for urban and territorial innovation. Discussed in dedicated essays in this book are novel approaches that connect experience with exploration, a new role for the creative and cultural sector in decarbonisation, and social innovation that merges activism, entrepreneurship, and public action. The use of studio work in the university as a "mirror" for theories and research follows at the end of this essay. In the outlook, further considerations for research in architecture and urbanism are offered.

Decarbonisation and cities

Nearly 40% of CO_2 emissions worldwide come from the construction, use, and demolition of buildings (UN 2020). Also other

ressource.architektur

Golden structural steel mats lifted into the air by steel frames, leaving an open space below: the installation ressource.architektur at the Real Estate Fair in Hanover transforms current debates on building and the city into a spatial experience. The nearly 3 tonnes of steel used for the installation is the amount per person needed for reinforced concrete in conventional new construction in the 400,000 new homes for which the federal government is aiming. For reinforced concrete alone, 6 tonnes of C02 are emitted per person. At the same time, Europe wants to become the first climate-neutral continent, is aiming for sustainable cities, is striving for a radical change in building with the New European Bauhaus and is just discovering the issue of sovereignty and security of production chains. How does this go together? ressource. architektur prominently addresses the redesign of cities through the creative reuse of existing buildings.

ressource.architektur was installed as a design build project by students from Leibniz Universität Hannover LUH and Hannover University of Applied Sciences HsH, jointly developed with the Chamber of Architects of Lower Saxony, the Association of German Architects BDA, Bund Deutscher Baumeister BDB, the Association of German Interior Architects BDIA, the Association of German Landscape Architects BDLA and the Building Culture Network of Lower Saxony, together with the Faculty of Architecture and Landscape at Leibniz University Hannover and the Interior Design course at Hannover University of Applied Sciences. ressource.architektur was supported by a large number of sponsors from the building industry. Design of the installation: Malin Osterheider, Max Passgang, Kimberly Rahn (all LUH), Paul Schomburg, Melanie Weber (HsH). Built with: Max Bender, Anna Bertram, Ferdinand Helmecke, Viviane Hilsenbeck, Lina Nikolic, Fabian Raue, Jannika Rehkopf, Helena Reinhard, Jean Sauerländer (all LUH), Vivian Ebeling, Lisa Faller, Vicky Frehe, Niklas Meyer, Amelie Miller, Antonia Reum, Niclas Thiry, Frithjof Wahl, Tessa Winkelmann (all HsH). Supervision: Prof. Jörg Schröder and Rebekka Wandt MSc (LUH), Prof. Bernd Rokahr and Prof. Tatjana Sabljo (HsH). Photo by Max Passgang.

CO_2-relevant topics are deeply linked to cities and living spaces, most prominently mobility. In order to make Europe the first climate-neutral continent, the European Green Deal needs to take these city-related topics into account. Several initiatives already address decarbonisation of buildings. For example, the EU strategy Renovation Wave (2020) aims at higher energy efficiency and decarbonisation through building renovation, and the EU strategic research and innovation partnership Built4People is addressing the sustainable transition of construction industries (2022) away from carbon. Security and sustainability, not only of the energy supply but also of material provision, production chains, and of the workforce, are further challenging factors.

The topic of social inclusion has gained additional importance due to high energy prices and inflation. Demand for housing is rising, and increasing social division is reviving the question of affordable housing and living. For example, of the 400,000 new housing units on the agenda of the German Federal Government, 100,000 are planned as social housing. However, sectoral initiatives and policies need to be set comprehensively in the context of urban transition towards sustainability. Current architectural and urban research highlights the importance of cities in the process of decarbonisation: cities are seen not only as a main stage where sectoral innovation and policies need to be coordinated, but also key to the acceleration of decarbonisation and increased quality of life for citizens through interaction and a sense of joint responsibility (Schröder 2020c). The EU Horizon mission for 100 cities to become climate-neutral by 2030 (2022b) is already addressing comprehensive cross-sectoral access to energy-efficient construction and renovation, sustainable mobility and decentralised energy production and storage. In a further step, a new focus on human-centred urban design and planning will be necessary, highlighting inclusion, empowerment, sharing, and activation, as well as new governance and financing models, and the broad and different aspects of digitalisation (JPI Urban Europe 2019). The innovative force—and, implicitly, the specific research approach—of the architectural and design disciplines is being addressed by the New European Bauhaus (European Commission 2022c), which calls for combining sustainability with aesthetics, technology with arts, and for an overall cultural change to realise climate neutrality.

Circular dynamics

Interest in circularity has been part of research into a shift towards sustainability since the 1990s (Camilleri 2018), when the open loops of linear material streams were detected as a major environmental problem and closed loops to contain human impact on natural ecosystems were proposed. In 2015, the EU introduced a Circular Economy Action Plan to foster resource- and energy-sensitivity and the use of renewable and natural resources as a field for work and business opportunities and competitiveness. Today, with the aim of the European Green Deal to accelerate decarbonisation and with the demand for secure and sustainable production chains, the shift to a circular economy has become even more important. At the same time, circularity principles are being further extended. The impulse of a circular economy is understood to induce a radical turn in the whole economic and societal system of cities (Ellen MacArthur Foundation, ARUP 2018) since, in the framework of a "performance economy" (Stahel, 2006), greater societal impact and value can be achieved.

The research project "Creative Food Cycles" (Schröder, 2019b), for example, offers an understanding of the topic of food as a cross-cutting field of innovation for a circular economy, leading to a redefinition of design approaches in multi-actor innovation processes. It identifies pathways to combine territorial resilience, entrepreneurial social practices, and technological innovation in order to operationalise linkages between a circular economy and society, culture, and space. The methodology follows the Ellen MacArthur Foundation's definition (2017) that a circular economy needs to realise innovation in three dimensions: first, to design out waste from production processes; second, to be regenerative by design; and third, to decouple growth from finite resource consumption. A focus on city-making, as implied in this essay, leads to the sharpening of these dimensions of a circular economy in culture and society: to design waste-less and carbon-free life cycles of buildings and cities, as well as to keep houses in use and good repair; to relate the regenerative dimension not only to nature (Giradet 2015) but also to cities and communities, disrupting concepts of urban regeneration that aim at a static vision instead of regenerative processual qualities (Schröder 2020a); and to use circular principles to secure and gain wellbeing and prosperity in inclusive, accessible, and affordable ways.

Based on this consideration, the term "circular dynamics" (Schröder 2021a) can express, on the one hand, the idea of creating dynamic processes that will also impact other sectors in the city and, on the other hand, the idea of bringing about a dynamic cultural, economic, and social shift, not least through breaking barriers between production and consumption and establishing new expressions, rituals, and aesthetics. Based on material cycles—and on a new awareness of material culture—the concept of circular dynamics extends to other flows that are necessary to generate sustainability in the city: flows of energy, flows of transport, financial/investment flows, flows of ideas, people, knowledge, abilities, culture, and values, and, not least, flows of space. The implication is, clearly, that cyclical thinking creates meaningful flows between local, supralocal, and global dimensions. It is about the overlapping, overlaying, and interference of cycles and flows from different sectors and scales, about fluidity and dynamics, and about bringing digital and material dimensions together. Thus, circular dynamics refers to open systems and "open habitats" (Schröder 2018) oriented towards sustainability—and to a networked idea of proximity and auto-sufficiency. Three examples can illustrate this definition: new financing and investment models (crowdfunding and sharing) not bound to a geographical border; new knowledge and research flows over distances; and multi-place living and working models that cross boundaries. Through addressing a multiplicity of flows, circular dynamics support systemic approaches to cities. They can trigger new perspectives on urban topics and establish coherent interrelations, for example between previously strictly separated perspectives on buildings—in a spatial-social and economic sense (building stocks), in a cultural sense (heritage), and in an ecological sense (resources)—towards a new logic of urban transformation for climate neutrality.

Circular territories
This essay now takes a territorial perspective in order to explore linkages between circularity, design, and city-making and to widen the spatial radius as well as the topical and methodological access. This entails including human living places beyond what is commonly defined as the city, i.e. an urban centre with more than 50,000 inhabitants. (Effectively, only 40% of Europeans live in cities; the other 60% reside in towns, suburbs, villages, smaller settlements linked into networks through cooperation, intersected by different forms of material and immaterial divisions and borders.) It also entails dynamic change due to parallel and contradictory processes of metropolisation, centralisation, extension, and diffusion of settlement (Soja 2012, Servillo 2016, Schröder 2017). At the same time, various forms of peripheries—urban, suburban, rural, remote—can be identified not only as a challenge for transition, but as a potential for overall sustainability and for innovation (Schröder et al. 2018).
Current new development of housing (mostly in small units) and industry zones is being applied to metropolitan agglomerations, but also to mid-sized cities and towns, leading to a current amount of about 60 hectares per day of new soil consumption in Germany: a major challenge for sustainability (Schröder 2020c). Furthermore, a territorial perspective can support the understanding of complex constellations formed by settlement patterns, infrastructures such as

transport and energy, and topography and natural factors and spaces, which are in constant flux. This complexity of constellations adds to the complexity of the task of territorial transformation towards sustainability and resilience (Viganò, Cavalieri 2019; Schröder 2020c). A territorial perspective based on concepts of urbanism has the advantage of offering a relational understanding of space (Secchi, Viganò 2009; Schröder 2017) in terms of changing interactions between space and society. It can support the understanding of the interplay of structural, material, imaginative as well as social, cultural, economic, ecological factors for analysis and for the projection of pathways of transformation. Relecting Castell's definition of a city "not [as] a framework, but a social practice in constant flux [...] a source of contradictions" (2005), the concept of space as an active agent (Schröder 2021b) allowing interaction between actors and space, as well as between values, cultural beliefs, lifestyles, is identified as playing an important role in territorial innovation processes.

Contributions to research into circularity in relation to territorial and urban transformation have come, until now, from three sides: first, concepts of resource and energy flows, which have been termed "urban metabolism" (van Timmeren 2014, Wachsmuth 2012, Grulois et al. 2018) or "circular cities" (Williams 2019, 2020) are addressed in a management and infrastructural approach, extended to eco-systemic thinking, the role of nature, ecological regeneration, and the topic of health (Furlan et al. 2022). Second, a circular economy is addressed in the context of economic development focused on circular business models, creative milieus and networks, upscaling, and innovation processes (Bourdin et al. 2021). Third, a circular approach to building construction for closed material cycles, disassembly methods, and so-called "urban mining" (Heisel, Hebel 2021) or the use of digital tools for the organisation of the material environment, setting up new market mechanisms and innovating public procurement in regard to used construction materials (Office Rotor, see Vanderstraeten 2021) are implying a decidedly passive understanding of the city. In most cases, circular approaches remain sectoral, very small-scale, and fixed on material questions, not including a broader vision of Circular Dynamics. In particular, more holistic approaches to territorial governance in conjunction with circularity and life-cycle-thinking are lacking (Amenta, Russo, van Timmeren, 2022, p. VI).

One of the few research contributions to conceptually link urban metabolism, circular economy, and territorial resilience proposes the concept of "circular land" for the Sicani area in Sicily (Carta 2017a, 2017b), stressing the necessary interaction between territorial governance, urbanism, and evaluation. If we understand human living places—settlements and the built environment—as the main stage for transformation, where different sectoral (and disciplinary) aspects converge, their future as "circular territories" needs to be based on circularity-activating concepts. Starting from an urbanistic and territorial perspective, such concepts can then contribute to creating development pathways (Schröder, Ferretti 2018), based on relational logics and the territorial potentials (and limitations) they need to take into consideration. To achieve a comprehensive approach to circular territories, economic, social, ecological, cultural, and spatial agency need to be combined, taking a people-centred view that starts from everyday life, living spaces, urban spaces, daily movements, economic activities, social and cultural factors and activities, and cultural beliefs, working with a relational understanding of space and actors. In the logic of a place-based approach to territorial policies (Barca et al. 2012), strategies, plans, and policies at different levels can then be effectively oriented towards circularity. The shift from the concept of mitigation of climate change to a focus on urban transformation towards resilience and sustainability (Wolfram 2016)—calling for systemic change—is giving importance to working with capacities of space and society for transformation. Adaptivity, redundancy, and robustness of strategies and tools in territorial governance can be identified as important qualities (Schröder 2021a). Based on these considerations, concepts towards circular territories can be articulated as space-oriented and actor-oriented.

Space-oriented concepts (space as active agent)

Circular spaces: A concept addressing the target of Net Zero Artificialisation (Schröder 2020b), preventing further extension and diffusion of urban structures, infrastructures, and social tissues, as well as eco-systemic and biodiversity damage. Circular spaces are those where soil-sealing (the destruction or covering of the ground with an impermeable material) is avoided, and thus contribute to circular transformation—possibly through market mechanisms similar to CO_2 certificates. They also consider the density and spatial qualities of newly built or re-built areas. Hence, this concept gives a decidedly new perspective to approaches to limit soil sealing or aiming at compactness over the last 20 years.

Circular transformation: A major concept for urban activation and intensification through urban projects under the Net Zero Artificialisation target. It aims to put circular objectives in the foreground and therefore to recycle areas and buildings beyond metropolitan centres; to think twice before tearing down existing buildings; to imagine and organise new, much more diffuse, systemic, small and large-scale

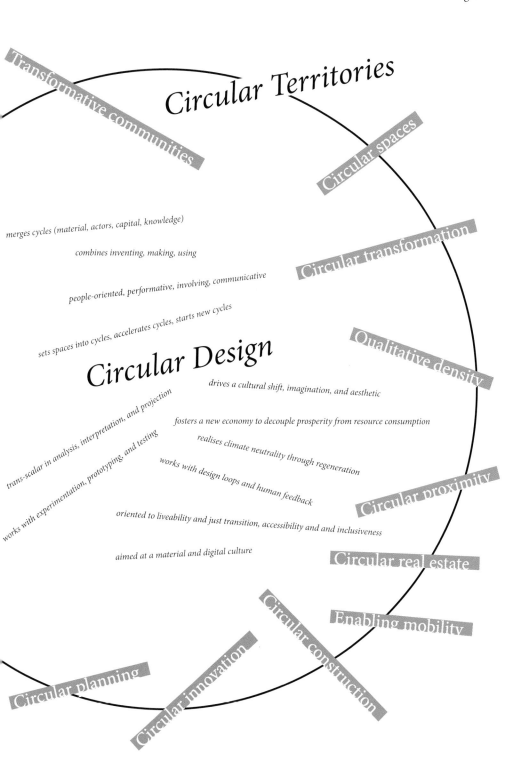

Transformative communities

Circular Territories

Circular spaces

Circular transformation

merges cycles (material, actors, capital, knowledge)

combines inventing, making, using

people-oriented, performative, involving, communicative

sets spaces into cycles, accelerates cycles, starts new cycles

Qualitative density

Circular Design

drives a cultural shift, imagination, and aesthetic

trans-scalar in analysis, interpretation, and projection

fosters a new economy to decouple prosperity from resource consumption

realises climate neutrality through regeneration

works with experimentation, prototyping, and testing

works with design loops and human feedback

Circular proximity

oriented to liveability and just transition, accessibility and and inclusiveness

aimed at a material and digital culture

Circular real estate

Enabling mobility

Circular planning

Circular innovation

Circular construction

forms of transformation strategies; and, in particular, to contribute to regenerative processes for places, economy, society, and nature. This not only means setting recycled buildings and areas into new multidimensional cycles, but supporting the acceleration of cycles, linking sectoral cycles, and even starting new cycles.

Qualitative density: A conceptual answer (Schröder 2021c) to current territorial concentration processes (not only in metropolitan centres, but also in smaller cities and towns) in order not to extend infrastructural systems. It is qualitative in relation to the territorial context (calling for new density models for urban fringes, smaller cities and towns) and in terms of fostering the advantages of social and cultural density for quality of life.

Circular proximity: This combines the targets of mixing (in functional and social composition, in activities over time), accessibility (in social terms and in regard to sustainable mobility) with social and cultural infrastructures and public spaces, and orients them towards circularity. It aims to contribute to new sustainable cycles and to use new cooperation and sharing models (e.g. in energy such as district heat-electricity provision and storage) or in the community, housing, or shared work spaces).

Enabling mobility: A concept to move into the foreground, not the transport infrastructure, but foot, bike and public transport, to consider the movements of people as well as the movement of goods, to use digital innovation and new electric technology, and to support circular transformation, qualitative density, and circular proximity, working with new life and work models, in particular for peripheries.

Actor-oriented concepts (for the activation of space)

Circular innovation processes: A concept to orient territorial innovation and traditional strategies in regional economic development towards circular sustainability and innovation, e. g. fostering business models, entrepreneurship, skills, knowledge, upscaling, innovative milieus and networks, targeted investments and financing, targeted clustering and links to research and education—and to coordinate with space-oriented concepts. And they aim to foster new roles for cultural and creative industries (CCI) as drivers of innovation in other sectors and for a cultural shift to sustainability.

Transformative communities: New organisational and financial forms of community organisation (co-working, co-living, prosumer models, community land trusts, etc.) that are oriented to foster and enhance sustainable transformation and to adopt circularity principles using digital innovation, sharing models, crowdfunding etc.

Circular construction economy: Oriented towards decarbonisation, energy-saving in all processes, use of renewable and natural materials, including a change in business models, entrepreneurship, clustering, procurement procedures, but also in knowledge, abilities, education, life-long learning for all involved actors.

Inclusive real estate: New sharing and ownership models, improved accessibility and inclusiveness that contribute to a circular access to urban and territorial development; new business models in real estate enhancing a circular economy (Ellen MacArthur Foundation 2021b).

Circular planning framework: The revision, adaptation, and extension of regulatory, legal, technical, and funding frameworks for a circularity-driven transformative approach to the built environment—a very critical point, since most of our regulatory background comes from and is still guided by the influence of modernist ideas, e.g. functional zoning, carbon-based engineering, and over-regulation.

Design for urban strategies and territorial governance

Already for the definition of these concepts for circular territories—and not just for their implementation—the character, role, and meaning of design for urban strategies and territorial governance needs to be revised. While design is a central element of theories in urbanism (i. e. urban design and planning), discussions about design are not really part of conventional planning theory, even if for several years traditional forms of plans have been replaced with more adaptive and integrative formats that adopt design approaches to organisational processes (e.g. Healy 2006; Neuman, Zonneveld 2021; Schröder 2021b). New participatory, activating, and cooperative approaches to policies, strategies, and projects are already referring to design thinking, even with the danger of provoking unrealistic expectations of participants in processes on urban and territorial scales under the label "co-design", which rely on a background of service-design theories (Wilson, Tewdwr-Jones 2022; Steen et al. 2011). Theories and concepts for spatial strategies and governance, with new tools such as contracts, stakeholder, and citizen involvement, cross-sectoral approaches, and decision support systems, offer several opportunities to include diverse concepts of design, ranging from service design to urban and architectural design.

A tentative framework for design in a territorial dimension (Schröder 2017) can be summarised in six dimensions:

- Explorative: systematic scenario building, e.g. adopting the agency and capacity of mapping as research tool (Schröder, Ferretti 2018; Corner 1999).
- Visionary: integrated and systematic design visions that interpret the existing structure and project towards desirable futures (Secchi, Viganò 2009; Phelps 2021).
- Coordinative: new formats and processes of spatial strategies, protocols, agendas (Schröder 2021b).
- Human-centred: the contribution of design in architecture and urbanism to place-based (Barca et al. 2012), site-specific (de Meulder, Marin, Shannon 2022) and human-centred factors in territorial governance.
- Multi-scalar: opening up information regarding development paths, spatial potentials, and limitations (Schröder, Ferretti 2018), not least referring to the concept of the "territory as palimpsest" (Corboz 2001), the understanding of territorial and urban contexts as historical layers.
- Projective: innovative projects—linked to places and space—for urban and territorial governance (Palermo, Ponzini 2010), and their interplay with processes of social interaction and decision-making (Steinitz 2012).

Circular design: background
The term "circular design" has been in use for several years in research and in the practice of product design, fashion, and furniture design, with a focus on the recycling of materials. A comprehensive overview in research is lacking; the literature offers quite limited sectoral and geographical studies, and only in a few cases is research into creating material cycles combined with new circular business models (e.g. in the field of fashion: Ellen MacArthur Foundation 2021a). IAAC in Barcelona can be seen as a frontrunner in relating Circular Design to architecture (Markopoulou 2019), with a strong technological and interdisciplinary cooncept, e. g. merging biological processes with building elements, inspired by the "cradle to cradle" concept (McDonough, Braungart 2002). At the same time, product design recalls its modernist vocation for a better life and better cities (Maldonado 2019) and promotes its role as a "strategic tool" for urban transition, equality, and quality of life (Helsinki City of Design). This includes the move from linear design—structuring information, finding the design solution, creating form—to iterative loops of design with human feedback, involving coding, programmes, protocols,

profiles, data analysis, but also new rituals, relations, desire, conflicts (Schröder 2021b). The approach of IAAC extends the conventional understanding of design as a limited part of architectural processes (the phase of drafting a concept) to design as an activity that includes making and works with models, prototypes, protocols—thus fabrication innovates design (and vice versa).

Design thinking, design research
"Design thinking" is a term that has become popular in management and economics in the last years. Linked mainly to theories of product and service design (Brown 2009), "design thinking" in this popular sense can be adopted to different sectors and tasks as a creative problem-solving approach that aims at positive impact and (disruptive) innovation. Its characteristics are the orientation to users and to outputs, commonly referred to as "solutions", and short iterative cycles of invention, realisation, and testing. "Design thinking" seems bound to specific cases; an "upscaling" of "solutions" is mostly understood as an aim to increase numbers and range. In this conventional form, design thinking remains a management technique. The relation of design to research is, in comparison, much sharper and clearly evolved in architecture and urbanism. As Nigel Cross puts it, architecture is to be understood as a "design discipline" (2012) characterised by "designerly ways of knowing and thinking". This definition overcomes the modernist impetus to "scientise" design. In the meantime, design research in architecture is established with adapted theory and transfer (Fraser 2013, Buchert 2014, Luce et al. 2022). It can be seen as the "missing link" in the specific constellation between theory and practice of the architectural disciplines, offering a theoretical framework for cognition-oriented, problem-oriented, and practice-related fundamental research. This is characteristic of the architectural disciplines, and of the specific multi-actor innovation ecosystems between academia, offices, and a broad range of stakeholders (public bodies, enterprises, civil society and cultural organisations).
Thus, the architectural disciplines have already developed a scientific understanding of design thinking that can be summarised in three points: First, a theoretical fundament is actively shaped, since "innovation lies in the convergence between the transformation of ideas and things" (Fagnoni 2016). Second, design thinking refers not only to "production" but also to "creation", in the sense of Aristotle's distinction between praxis and poiesis (Jaeger 1957), thus addressing a decidedly larger range of values. And third, design thinking addresses space and context, and thus the ability to comprehensively bundle and merge a multiplicity of sectoral, scalar, and social aspects is a major characteristic. It is the synthesising power of

architectural design thinking that makes it particularly appealing and effective for transforming the complexity of cities and territories, not only as systems, but also as spaces (Schröder 2021a)—hence, as material as well as a cultural and social construction (Rossi 1966). Similar to the realisation of the last years—due to the challenge of climate change—that architecture is in fact a research discipline—created academically for urban expansion in the nineteenth century—its common and self-understanding as creative discipline is changing radically. Architecture was once seen as the creation of something new. Now, we follow the mission "to recycle is to design", as Mosè Ricci (2016) wrote. The impact of this shift not only for architects themselves but for the common image of architecture could not be more disruptive. And it is not only about using recycled materials or converting existing buildings ("re-use", Stockhammer 2021): the novelty lies in setting them into meaningful cycles and creating new cycles towards sustainability—the major conceptual result of the Italian National Research project PRIN "Re-Cycle" (Ricci, Schröder 2016; Schröder et al. 2017). Effectively, if we seriously aim to create circular spaces with net-zero soil consumption and the circular transformation of cities, it is quite clear that we have to overcome the strong traditional borders between new construction and renovation/conversion in research and practice, mindsets, and ways of acting. For everything they do, architects will always need to combine their knowledge and abilities to work with the existing as well as to add, transform and extend with new spatial ideas. The creative mission of circular design is to install space. Obviously, this comprehensive and holistic approach contradicts the ongoing specialisation in the architectural disciplines. In this sense, circular design is a call to valorise, research, teach, and learn the comprehensive and strategic qualities of architectural thinking and work with new eyes.

Circular design towards circular territories
As a working definition, circular design seeks innovative ways to set space into cycles towards sustainability, and to contribute towards circular territories as a paradigm for urbanism and architecture, but also as an impulse for discussions in other design fields, in territorial governance, and in collaboration with other disciplines and society.

Thus circular design
1. combines processes of inventing, making, and using
2. is people-oriented, performative, involving, communicative
3. sets spaces in sustainable cycles, accelerates cycles, starts new cycles
4. connects sectoral cycles

5. is trans-scalar in analysis, interpretation, and projection
6. works with design loops and human feedback
7. includes experimentation, prototyping, and testing
8. aims at a combined material and digital culture
9. is oriented to liveability, accessibility, and inclusion
10. realises climate neutrality through regeneration (for places, communities, and nature)
11. fosters a new economy and decouples well-being from finite resource consumption
12. drives a cultural shift, imagination, and aesthetics.

Clearly, for this conceptual vision we will have to develop not only non-linear design processes but also new tools for circular processes. These tools will be more interactive and communicate, will work with early tests and prototyping, human feedback, new forms of strategies, digital methods in different dimensions, new ways of organising resources, knowledge, and abilities in urban and architectural processes with many stakeholders. For the territorial level of circular design, tools such as mapping, visions, and scenarios have already been mentioned. Infographics and diagrams, data interpretation, working with unconventional and open data, as well as videos and artistic approaches are also ongoing fields of innovation, overlaying digital and material methods and outputs. As underlying concepts, narratives (Schröder 2020d) can bridge personal and cultural views in analysis, projection, visioning, transformation processes, and communication (see the essay about Circular Narratives on p. 30).

Mirroring with studio projects
The discussion of circular design in this outline and in the other essays in the book is mirrored in the second part of the book by selected studio projects at the university. This mirroring has been a vivid and stimulating experience for us researchers when exploring topics and places and discussing and sharpening approaches and concepts together with our students while guiding their work. Design thinking in architecture and urban design stands as studio project in itself, with a design research orientation in its concepts and methodologies. It has led us to ask about the innovations in teaching, content, formats, and methods, that we can draw from research. In this sense, the book shows the outcomes of involving students in university teaching, in particular in a strong orientation to design research and interdisciplinary linkages for their future in academia and in practice. This second part of the book features case studies from all over Europe (and beyond) that in different ways express and articulate ideas about circular design. In a certain sense, it is a protocol for a joint

discovery process. Sixteen studio projects and thesis projects (selected from more than 200 that we have supervised over the last three years) are shown through a small part of their overall volume. Experimental graphic expression and communication—which we consider fundamental—is interwoven with discussions about focus, objectives, methodologies, and evaluation. All projects start from existing cities and territories and from existing innovative initiatives that are close to the "circular transformation" concept. Even if some of the projects seem more utopic than others—and in fact, disruptive thinking is one of the aims—they all precisely tag questions, actors, initiatives, trends, and movements in place. The projects are organised into chapters according to studio topics (Medways, Seaside, Mountains, New Bauhaus City) or are arranged into categories such as New Systems, New Processes, Transformation. Between the essays and the projects, the chapter "Interface" offers a taxonomy of the projects, installed retrospectively, which links them to the theoretical framework and which can serve to access themes, strategies, tools, and places.

Outlook

Since this essay is an outline for a circular design paradigm towards circular territories, it is necessarily open and inconclusive. In accordance with the multiple culture of innovation in architecture, based on a multiplicity of actors, it aims to activate dynamic fields and networks of ideas, people, and space oriented to circular principles—targeting urban and territorial sustainability, climate resilience, and climate neutrality. Circular design can innovate architecture and urban design and planning and enhance new linkages with other design, creative, and artistic disciplines. At the same time, the outline can be read as a research manifesto calling for new projects, publications, exhibitions, prototypes, collaboration. It also calls for a further examination of how a circular design paradigm can contribute to sharpening concepts of design research, and for designerly ways of researching in a cognition-oriented, performative, and transferable way. Thus, circular design, inspired by and working with the interaction of space and society, could help (re-)establish fundamental research in architecture (Luce et al. 2022) precisely because societal questions urge the development of open and free research.

Bibliography:

Amenta L., Russo M., van Timmeren A., eds. (2022) *Regenerative Territories. Dimensions of circularity for healthy metabolisms.* Cham, Springer.

Barca F., McCann P., Rodríguez-Pose A. (2012) "The Case for regional development intervention: Place-based versus place-neutral approaches". In: *Journal of Regional Science,* vol. 52 (2012), issue 1, pp. 134–152.

Bourdin S., Galliano D., Gonçalves A. (2021) "Circularities in territories: opportunities and challenges". In: *European Planning Studies*. DOI: https://doi.org/10.1080/09654313.2021.197 3174.

Brown T. (2009) *Change by Design: How design thinking transforms organisations and inspires innovation*. New York, Harper Business.

Buchert M., ed. (2014) *Design and Research in Architecture*. Berlin, JOVIS.

Built4People (2022) *Built4People Partnership: Strategic research and innovation agenda*. Available online at: http://ec.europa.eu/info/sites/default/files/research_and_innovation/funding/documents/ec_rtd_he-partnerships-built4people-agenda.pdf (01.06.2022).

Camilleri M. A. (2018) "The circular economy's closed loop and product service systems for sustainable development: A comprehensive review and appraisal". In: *Sustainable Development* 27(1).

Carta M. (2017a) "Pianificare il territorio circolare, governare lo sviluppo locale". In: Carta M., Contato C., Orlando M., eds. (2017) *Pianificare l'innovazione locale. Strategie e progetti per lo sviluppo locale creativo: l'esperienza del SicaniLab*, Milano, Franco Angeli, pp. 13–25.

Carta M. (2017b) *The Augmented City. A Paradigm Shift*. Trento/Barcelona, ListLab.

Castells M., Cardoso G., eds. (2005) *The Network Society: From Knowledge to Policy*. Washington, Johns Hopkins Center for Transatlantic Relations.

Corboz A. (2001) *Le Territoire comme palimpseste et autres essais*. Besancon: Les éditions de l'imprimeur (first published 1983).

Corner J. (1999) *Recovering Landscape*. New York, Princeton Architectural Press.

Creative Denmark (2021) *Designing the irresistible circular society. White paper*. Available online at: http://cms.creativedenmark.com/media/Creative-Denmark_white-paper_Designing-the-irresistible-circular-society.pdf (01.06.2022).

Cross N. (2012) "From a design science to a design discipline: Understanding designerly ways of knowing and thinking". In: Michel R., ed. (2012) *Design Research Now: Essays and Selected Projects*. Berlin/Boston, Birkhäuser, pp. 41–54.

De Meulder B., Marin J., Shannon K. (2022) "Evolving Relations of Landscape, Infrastructure and Urbanization Toward Circularity: Flanders and Vietnam". In: Amenta L., Russo M., van Timmeren A., eds. (2022) *Regenerative Territories. Dimensions of Circularity for Healthy Metabolisms*. Cham, Springer, pp. 107–121.

Ellen MacArthur Foundation, ARUP (2018) *Circular Economy in Cities. Project Guide*. Available online at: http://www.ellenmacarthurfoundation.org/assets/downloads/CE-in-Cities-Project-Guide_Mar19.pdf (01.06.2022).

Ellen MacArthur Foundation (2021a) *Circular Design for Fashion*. Cowes, Ellen MacArthur Foundation.

Ellen MacArthur Foundation (2021b) *Realising the value of circular economy in real estate*. Available online at: http://ellenmacarthurfoundation.org/articles/realising-the-value-of-the-circular-economy-in-real-estate (01.06.2022).

Ellen MacArthur Foundation (2017) *Cities in the Circular Economy: An initial exploration*. Available online at: http://ellenmacarthurfoundation.org/cities-in-the-circular-economy-an-initial-exploration (01.06.2022).

Espon (2020) Espon SUPER. Sustainable Urbanisation and land-use Practices in European Regions. Luxembourg, Espon. Avaliable Online at: https://ec.europa.eu/regional_policy/rest/cms/upload/24082020_125113_espon_super_final_report_annex_5___handbook.pdf (01.06.2022).

European Commission, Directorate-General for Internal Market, Industry, Entrepreneurship, and SMEs (2022a) *Buildings and Construction*. Available online at: http://ec.europa.eu/growth/industry/sustainability/buildings-and-construction_en (01.06.2022).

European Commission (2022b) *Commission announces 100 cities participating in EU Mission for climate-neutral and smart cities by 2030*. Press release. Available online at: https://ec.europa.eu/commission/presscorner/detail/en/IP_22_2591 (01.06.2022).

European Commission, Directorate-General for Research and Innovation (2022c) *Horizon Europe – New European Bauhaus Nexus Report*. DOI: http://data.europa.eu/doi/10.2777/49925.

European Commission (2020) *A Renovation Wave for Europe: greening our buildings, creating jobs, improving lives*. COM(2020) 662. Available online at: http://eur-lex.europa.eu/resource.html?uri=cellar:0638aa1d-0f02-11eb-bc07-01aa75ed71a1.0003.02/DOC_1&format=PDF (01.06.2022).

Eurostat (2020) *Energy, transport, and environment statistics. 2020 edition.* Available online at: http://ec.europa.eu/eurostat/documents/3217494/11478276/KS-DK-20-001-EN-N.pdf/06d-daf8d-1745-76b5-838e-013524781340?t=1605526083000 (01.06.2022).

Fagnoni R. (2016) "Core values for ReCycle Social Innovators". In: Ricci M., Schröder J., eds. (2016) *Towards a Pro-active Manifesto.* PRIN ReCycle Series, New Life Cycles for Architectures and Infrastructures of City and Landscape. Rome, Aracne Editrice, pp. 30–45.

Fraser M., ed. (2013) *Design Research in Architecture: An overview.* Chichester, Ashgate.

Furlan C., Wandl A., Cavalieri C., Munoz Unceta P. (2022) "Territorialising Circularity". In: Amenta L., Russo M., van Timmeren A., eds. (2022) *Regenerative Territories. Dimensions of Circularity for Healthy Metabolisms.* Cham, Springer, pp. 31–50.

Girardet, H. (2015) *Creating Regenerative Cities.* London, Taylor & Francis.

Gruloi, G., Tosi M. C., Crosas C., eds. (2018) *Designing Territorial Metabolism:.Brussels, Barcelona, and Veneto.* Berlin, JOVIS.

Healy P. (2006) *Urban Complexity and Spatial Strategies: a relational planning for our times.* London, Routledge.

Heisel F., Hebel D. E., eds. (2021) *Urban Mining und kreislaufgerechtes Bauen. Die Stadt als Rohstofflager.* Stuttgart, Fraunhofer IRB Verlag.

Jaeger W., ed. (1957) *Aristotelis Metaphysica.* Oxford, Oxford Classical Texts, VI E 1025b18–1026a19.

JPI Urban Europe (2019) *Urban Europe Strategic Research and Innovation Agenda 2.0.* Available online at: http://jpi-urbaneurope.eu/wp-content/uploads/2019/02/SRIA2.0.pdf (01.06.2022).

Luce M., Pfarr-Harfst M, Reeh J., Schröder J., Tessmann O. (2022) *Forschungsexzellenz in der Architektur : Standards zur Bewertung und Förderung der Forschung in den Architekturfachbereichen der Technischen Universitäten in Deutschland (TU9).* Hannover, Institutionelles Repositorium der Leibniz Universität Hannover. DOI: http://doi.org/10.15488/11827.

Maldonado T. (2019) *Design, Nature, and Revolution.* Minneapolis: University of Minnesota Press (Orig. La speranza progettuale, 1970).

Markopoulou A. (2019) "Disrupting through Circular Design". In: Markopoulou A., ed. (2019) *Responsive Cities: Disrupting through Circular Design.* Barcelona, IAAC Institute of Advanced Architecture, pp. 12–19.

McDonough W., Braungart M. (2002) *Cradle to Cradle: Remaking the Way We Make Things.* New York: North Point Press.

Neuman M., Zonneveld W. (2021) *The Routledge Handbook of Regional Design.* London, Routledge.

Palermo P. C., Ponzini D. (2010) *Spatial Planning and Urban Development: critical perspectives.* London, Springer.

Phelps N. A. (2021) *The Urban Planning Imagination: A Critical International Introduction.* Hoboken, Wiley.

Ricci M. (2016) "The ReCycle GOA Pro-active Manifesto". In: Ricci M., Schröder J., eds. (2016) *Towards a Pro-active Manifesto.* PRIN ReCycle series, New life cycles for architectures and infrastructures of city and landscape. Rome, Aracne Editrice, pp. 21–29.

Rossi A. (1966) *L'architettura della città.* Padova, Marsilio.

Sannolo A., Bocchino C., De Rosa D. (2020) "Zéro Artificialisation Nette Target: towards circular cities and territories". In: *Sustainable Mediterranean Construction* 2020/12, pp. 194–193.

Schröder J. (2022) *ressource.architektur: Design Build Projekt für die Real Estate Arena 2022.* Available online at: http://www.staedtebau.uni-hannover.de/fileadmin/staedtebau/Regionales_Bauen_und_Siedlungsplanung/Download/ressource.architektur.pdf (01.06.2022).

Schröder J. (2021a) "Territorialising Resilience: Innovation Processes for Circular Dynamics". In: Carta M., Perbellini M.R., Lara-Hernandez J. A., eds. (2022) *Resilient Communities and the Peccioli Charter.* Cham, Springer, pp. 71–84.

Schröder J. (2021b) "Cosmopolitan Design". In: Schröder J., Carta M., Scaffidi F., Contato A., eds. (2021) *Cosmopolitan Habitat. A research agenda for urban resilience.* Berlin, JOVIS, pp. 12–16.

Schröder J. (2021c) "Design-led resilience pathways for places beyond metropolis". In: Schröder J., Cappeller R., eds. (2021) *New Bauhaus City. Rediscovering territories outside of metropolis.* Hannover, Regionales Bauen und Siedlungsplanung, pp. 9–16.

Schröder J. (2021d) "New Habitat Explorations". In: Schröder J., Diesch A., eds. (2021) *Mountains. Habitat Explorations.* Hannover, Regionales Bauen und Siedlungsplanung, pp. 7–9.

Schröder J. (2020a) "Circular Design for the Regenerative City: A Spatial-digital Paradigm". In: Schröder J., Sommariva E., Sposito S., eds. (2020) *Creative Food Cycles - Book 1.* Hannover, Regionales Bauen und Siedlungsplanung, pp. 17–31.

Schröder J. (2020b) "Climate Commons. Circular Design für neue Siedlungsmodelle". In: Schröder J., Diesch A., eds. (2019) *Climate Commons.* Hannover, Regionales Bauen und Siedlungsplanung, pp. 9–17.

Schröder J. (2020c) "Peripheries—Dynamics for the Green Deal". In: *Topos,* special issue 2020, urbanes.land. Available online at: http://urbanesland.toposmagazine.com/client_articles/peripheries-dynamics-for-the-green-deal (01.06.2022).

Schröder J. (2020d) "Urban Narratives". In: Schröder J., Cappeller R., eds. (2020) *Cosmopolitan Habitat: Urban Narratives.* Hannover, Regionales Bauen und Siedlungsplanung, pp. 6–7.

Schröder J. (2019a) "Circular Design and the Paradigm of Gestaltung in Creative Food Cycles". In: Markopoulou A., ed. (2019) *Responsive Cities: Disrupting through Circular Design.* Barcelona, IAAC Institute of Advanced Architecture, pp. 24–27.

Schröder J. (2019b) "Creative Food Cycles towards Urban Futures and Circular Economy". In: Markoupoulou A., Farinea C., Ciccone F., Marengo M., eds. (2019) *Food Interactions Catalogue.* Barcelona, IAAC Institute of Advanced Architecture of Catalonia, pp. 9–15.

Schröder J., Carta M., Ferretti M., Lino B., eds. (2018) *Dynamics of Periphery. Atlas of Emerging Creative and Resilient Habitats.* Berlin, JOVIS.

Schröder J., Ferretti M. (2018) *Scenarios and Patterns for Regiobranding.* Berlin, JOVIS.

Schröder J. (2017) "Towards an Architecture of Territories". In: Schröder J., Carta M., Ferretti M., Lino B., eds. (2016) *Territories: Rural-urban Strategies.* Berlin, JOVIS, pp. 14–33.

Schröder J., Ferretti M., Hartmann S., Sommariva E. (2017) "ReCycle: A territory-based approach". In: Fabian L., Munarin S., eds. (2017) *ReCycle Italy Atlante.* Syracuse, LetteraVentidue, pp. 385–387.

Secchi B., Viganò P. (2009) *Territory of a New Nodernity.* Antwerp, Centraal Boekhuis.

Servillo L., Atkinson R., Hamdouch A. (2016) "Small and medium-sized towns in Europe: conceptual, methodological, and policy issues". In: *Tijdschift voor Economische en Sociale Geografie,* 2017. Dutch Royal Geographic Society.

Soja E. (2012) "Regional Urbanisation and the End of the Metropolis Era". In: Bridge G., Watson S., eds. (2012) *The New Blackwell Companion to the City.* Oxford, Blackwell, pp. 679–689.

Stahel W. (2006) *The Performance Economy.* New York, Palgrave Macmillan.

Steen M., Manschot M., De Koning N. (2011) "Benefits of Co-design in Service Design Projects". In: *International Journal of Design,* 5(2), 53–60.

Steinitz C. (2012) *A Framework for Geodesign. Changing Geography by Design.* Aylesbury, Esri.

Stockhammer D. (2021) *Upcycling. Reuse and Repurposing as a Design Principle in Architecture.* Liechtenstein, Triest Verlag.

UN Environment Programme (2020) *2020 Global Status Report for Buildings and Construction.* Available online at: http://globalabc.org/sites/default/files/inline-files/2020%20Buildings%20GSR_FULL%20REPORT.pdf (01.06.2022).

Vanderstraeten M., Ghyoot M., Naval S., Geerts G. (2021) "Réemployer des matériaux de construction dans les marchés publics". In: *Chronique des marchés publics,* 2020-21, pp. 599–616.

Van Timmeren A. (2014) *The Concept of the Urban Metabolism* (UM). Delft, Delft Technical University.

Viganò P., Cavalieri C., eds. (2019) *The Horizontal Metropolis: A radical project.* Zürich, Park Books.

Wachsmuth D. (2012) "Three Ecologies: Urban Metabolism and the Society-Nature Opposition". In: *The Sociological Quarterly.* Vol. 53 (2012), issue 3, pp. 506–523.

Williams J. (2021) *Circular Cities: A Revolution in Urban Sustainability.* London, Routledge.

Williams J. (2019) "Circular Cities". In: *Urban Studies,* 56(13), 2746–2762.

Wilson A., Tewdwr-Jones M. (2022) *Digital Participatory Planning: Citizen engagement, democracy, and design.* London, Routledge.

Wolfram M. (2016) "Conceptualizing Urban Transformative Capacity: A framework for research and policy". In: *Cities* 51, pp. 121–130.

Circular Narratives

Riccarda Cappeller

Going on a journey—whether an imaginative-fictional or a real-time travelling of space, time, and people—is always about making discoveries on the move. It is about sequences of images, created through different kinds of storytelling, characters, or the memories and impressions gathered by being in spaces, observing, and interacting with them. Georges Perec in "Species of Spaces and other Pieces" (1974) introduces a practical exercise to record a street, teaching the reader how to see and take notice of a situation through asking questions and describing happenings, the time passing, or people moving. It is a moment—a setting—as if it were a stage and the reader and Perec are transferred into the same dimension, becoming flaneurs, wanderers, or storytellers, following the concept discussed by Georg Simmel in *Die Großstadt und das Geistesleben* (1903; The Metropolis and Mental Life) or of Walter Benjamin in *Städtebilder* (1963; City Images).

As a form of empirical research with a creative approach, the journey can be used to read urban situations make and share discoveries, visually and conceptually binding together diverse types of information. At the same time, it allows one to move from one place or scale to another, opening the possibility to engage with specific aspects or the experience as a whole. "Space in this sense is used as a tool and medium to transfer complexities and share narratives" (Cappeller 2020). It invites us to change our perception and way of making sense of urban situations, working with the multiplicity of inherent perspectives and taking a step back to reflect on its relations.

Based on these first thoughts, this essay examines a possible understanding of what circular narratives could mean. It uses the research-oriented design projects presented later in this book as a theoretically grounded and—as urban design exercises—practically evolved background. These projects allow the discussion of a new "narrative creation" in urban design that integrates interdisciplinary and multi-scalar approaches to make the design processes graspable. Departing from the very personal interest of their creators, the projects, which deal with very different places and topics, give an overview of current discussions, urban transformation processes,

This essay looks at how complex relations in topics of circularity can be put together and transferred to a broader public. The creation of narratives for existent spaces, the thinking-making in design processes, and the cultural dimension of urban space are theoretically discussed and supported with examples using artistic approaches. The aim is to open the urban design perspective and emphasise a situated knowledge creation.

and repeatedly appearing needs for new forms of social and spatial interaction, showing conceptually strong strategies for creating more open, dense, or mixed living spaces. This essay goes a step further and includes approaches from other disciplines that have innovative potential and can contribute to urban design as "integrative field of study, profession and course of action [that] takes a clear stance for inter- and transdisciplinary co-production as well as for a systemic understanding of [contemporary urban] challenges" (Giseke et al. 2021).

Circular narratives emphasise the creation of situated knowledge or context-related readings and writings of space that connect to existing situations or happenings and aim at deep analysis. They take a distance from a more theoretical-fictional imagination not bound to any specific location, and look at the intersection of the transformation and performativity of space and the agency of architects and urban designers. Three research targets are foregrounded:

- The characterisation of *Circular Narratives* as inventive and artistic approaches to communicate and transfer the complexity of urban transformation processes.
- The definition of thinking-making in a research-oriented design practice as narrative creation.
- The cultural understanding of space as a make-shift phenomenon, detecting the power of existing spatial resources in order to link concepts of semiotics with circularity.

Each of these targets is combined with an example of a narrative. They introduce artistic approaches as form of knowledge production (Borgdorff 2010), that deal with transferring the complexity of urban space and offer alternative formats to narrate the hidden values of existing situations and the process of designing. "Artistic practices can alter perception and aesthetic parameters, recognize potential and put into effect, formulate opposing positions, address and test alternative lifestyles, question existing power relations, and strengthen and create synergies" (Keitz, Meyer in Finkenberger et al. 2019, p. 60). They help to develop curiosity, redefine problems, experiment and learn by doing, while reflecting these processes. The journeys referred to as examples combine pragmatic, tangible "hard facts" with aesthetic and more emotional sensations, and connect to Zardini's consideration (2006) that "critical thinking is no longer driven by language, semiotics, text and signs, but by a rediscovery of phenomenology, experience, the body, perception, and the senses". Through the active engagement of the visitor or reader, as in the case of Perec, the examples generate knowledge, test, and critically reflect on it. The on-site installations and "Situated Drawings" by Public Works, the design research course "Scenes" at Leibniz University Hannover, as well as the documentary theatre play "Großbaustelle" by Rimini Protokoll, are briefly explained and visualised in a conceptual way, connecting to the research targets. Their value lies not only in the stories they tell, but in the forms of collective creation, knowledge generation, and complex urban transformation processes they trigger or thematise.

How Circular Narratives transfer the complexity of urban transformation processes
Addressing circularity in urban design processes opens the question of how to think, create, and realise the complexity of future living spaces, integrating a view of the "streams and flows not only of materials, but also of space, networks, ideas, knowledge, organised in overlapping, interactive, and reciprocal cycles" (Schröder 2022). It is about recycling, reusing, and reprogramming the existing space and

taking into consideration the current challenges we are facing as society: the topics of climate change, energy sufficiency, and decarbonisation, the need for solutions for crises in the housing market, but also migration flows, social and political inequality, and the resulting segregation that has even increased due to the pandemic. The expectation towards urban design, today, as discussed in the framework of the New European Bauhaus, is about conscious decision-making, mission-oriented innovation, reworking cultures that shape public life, the act of prototyping, creating tangible experiences of everyday life, and producing new ways of seeing and doing. There is a "necessity to create new forms of representation and visual media to visualise the process of design" (Schnell et al. 2016). Circular narratives, here, enter as new approaches and formats to research, analyse, and transmit urban complexities. They address the creation of regenerative territories and the responsible and sustainable action of designers. Dealing with urban complexity as a potential, and fostering a positioning through a democratic and cultural agency, connects urban design with architecture. It is a comprehensive understanding and communication of space where the "journey" that links different examples and topics of the urban realm is a key element. This consideration builds upon the long tradition of routes and itineraries from the eighteenth century, the Grand Tour, where young, upper-class men, like Alexander von Humboldt, travelled around the world. His visual representations perfectly show how the personal impressions and scientific findings of these journeys were gathered and brought together as observations and reflected on in writings.

But what exactly do we mean by narratives in urban design? Why are they important for innovation and in what way can they help us to understand urban life as an "irreducible product of mixture" (Amin, Thrift 2008) in constant transformation? Narratives, in general, are "ways of presenting or understanding a situation or series of events that reflect and promote a particular point of view or set of values" (Merriam-Webster). They are stories that draw together, densify, and organise all kinds of information, mediating them as experiences in textual or visual, sometimes also mixed formats, such as maps, films, collages, documentary films, or comics. Narratives create relations between fact and emotion, provide means to make sense of and understand social phenomena and individual experiences (Bond, Thompson-Fawcett 2008). They plot cities through language (Wirth-Nesher 1996, p. 4) and they are able to bring together an analytical-interpretative and a conceptual-projective perspective that fosters transformative aspects in order to analyse and understand (Ferretti 2019) territories, their material and immaterial components, as well as subjective experiences. Creating different and critical perspectives on territories is about new insights that bundle and examine "urbanistic know-how, critical reflection, and artistic exploration" (Schröder 2021). Narratives in this sense work as strategic tools for the practice of design and starting points to generate debates (Ferretti 2019, p. 106). They are representations of both the dialogical thinking processes happening within the designer's head (Rittel 1992, p. 136) and the site-specific aspects or experiences with which the designer deals. Focusing on the creation and transformation of our habitats calls for a more open design approach "that is exploratory and adaptive and responds to given conditions" (Langner in Giseke et al. 2021), creating new possibilities for improvising in and experimenting with the already built spaces. This places a focus on the performativity of urban situations (Wolfrum 2015), capturing the logic of the actions through heterogeneous media and techniques (Schnell et al. 2016). It requires a conscious positioning of the designer, as introduced by Schön with the "Reflexive Practitioner" (1983), and a deep analysis based on ethnographic and anthropological approaches (Roberts 2016). As Wirth-Nesher argues, "the 'real city' cannot be experienced without mediation" (1996, p. 10). (Urban) designers, as the "skilled understanders" (Ward 1996, p. 17), therefore have to be able to imagine and communicate the possible potential of future living spaces. As introduced with the concept of "As Found" by Alison and Peter Smithson, described by Schregenberger and Lichtenstein (2001), it is an approach to the practice of designing that links arts and science. Calling for a dynamic process of knowledge creation, we need to engage with and recognise the value of the existing space, following its traces with interest (ibid.) and make it accessible to a broader audience. Putting the experience of everyday life first is the departure point for an inventive activity: "the addressing of a method [...] to a specific problem and the capacity of what emerges in the use of that method to change the problem" (Lury, Wakeford, 2012, p. 7).

The thinking-making of design research practices as narrative creation
If we recognise the "value of design in its development" (Cross 2006, p. 25) and the process of its creation and its knowledge as existing in the products it creates, we—as the creators, designers, and craftsmen of architectural and urban spaces—have to interrogate the situations with which we are dealing. We also have to make our experience and knowledge of them apparent. The multiple forms of "designerly ways of knowing" (Cross 2006, p. 1) and working with the built environment as both tool and medium (Cappeller 2020) represent the active

and generative agency of design. They connect to the idea of the architect and theorist Stan Allen that "to recognise and accept the mixed character of architecture's [urban] procedures" (2000, p. XXIV) "requires multiple tactics of exposition" (ibid.). In the research-oriented design projects presented in this book we can see various visual expressions of different working steps, such as maps and infographics, combining analytical and conceptual aspects, programmatic schemes and outlines of processual projections or images and collages for the creation of scenarios and visions. Here, mixed approaches in the process of analysing—searching, developing ideas, inventing, testing, and developing them further—and the representation of a possible integration of the created ideas in the particular spatial situations selected by each of the authors, plays an important role. Reading the city as a cultural dimension puts to the forefront the complex and constantly shifting relationships that express the need for urban design to deal with the unexpected through questions about permanence and the collective character of the city, defined in a specific time and through society—as already mentioned by Aldo Rossi in his Architecture of the City (1982). A design process can be compared to scientific research processes by following the main steps of a research cycle: it starts with a concrete experience or question—the analysis of a spatial situation, followed by a reflective observation that helps to form an abstract conceptualisation—the selection of topics relevant for a situation and their relation to first ideas. As a next step, these first and more abstract assumptions are further discussed, developed, and situated in a larger context, before moving towards an active testing and experimentation phase—the realisation and implementation of ideas on various scales that are then evaluated. In the act of designing, these phases on the one hand follow each other, but on the other hand, at each stage, allow a jump back or forth, automatically integrating multiple testing and feed-back loops before coming to a concrete proposal. It is an open process that, without knowing the result beforehand, allows a constant transformation and re-definition of the topic worked on. Following Cross's concept of "designerly ways of knowing", this process combines the understanding of a problem and alternatives to answer it. A profound creation of awareness and of "cognition" of all the influential components is essential to create innovation.

A cultural perspective and understanding of urban space as a make-shift phenomenon

"The transfer of urban space is grounded in semiotics, where its elements and connective structures are seen as signs or set of signs" (Ameel 2016). In the 1980s, Roland Barthes made apparent the

City as classroom

Platform cafe

"Situated Drawings" by Public Works

Acting in various urban situations, the art and architecture office Public Works has developed "Situated Drawings" as a "representational device [for] a series of micro activist performances" (Lang 2019) and form of direct communication. Building upon place-specific learning in live projects and a relational understanding of space, it is a critique of existing architectural representation. Discovered through and with the users of a particular space, local knowledge and skills, fragmented experiences, multiple views upon the area, and personal stories are brought together in "spatialised collages", sharing and critically reflecting on what constitutes the place. These spaces of engagement and informal learning are created together with local actors, dealing with different kinds of complexities, understanding knowledge as a transversal category that emerges through being situated, and building on the practice of collaborative and informal making (Lang 2019). The collages are similar to tableaus vivants (living pictures) that work as a "depiction of a scene usually presented on stage" (Merriam-Webster). Intentionally they are both artistic forms and expressions of coexistence and temporality, and they tell many stories at the same time.

The farm

Grove Adventure Playground

Situated Drawing "A Public Land Grab" by Public Works. Image: courtesy of Public Works "need of a new scientific energy to transform […] data [in this case space-related data] and shift from metaphor to description of signification" (1986). Such a detailed description also entails the interpretation of space and makes its cultural dimension and immaterial value accessible. It depends on the individual perception, concepts, memories, and ideas connected to each spatial situation that, in relation to people's different mindsets, offer multiple kinds of readings that can greatly differ from each other. In this context, Barthes understands narratives as metaphors and the city as speaking a language. Having the ability to read and write the city, (urban) designers can act as mediators, facilitating interaction and communication, becoming storytellers of their own design-research journeys. They do not only transmit a materialised vision of the future, but also communicate their way of experiencing, understanding, and working with it, often revealing an insatiable desire to learn.

Dealing with the scenery, the dramaturgy, and mental spaces (Baudrillard 1999) designers become creators of narratives and foster a more comprehensive understanding of space as a source of inspiration. Placing existing spatial resources at the centre of discussion characterises them as integrative elements that, through collective memories and the materialised visions of past societies, bring flows of people and materials together and confront the reader with questions around the past, present, and future. Moreover, they call for different approaches and processes of transformation, for political and social support and public engagement in testing and experimenting with spatial ideas and models of co-living, co-learning, co-working, and co-creation, as well as the setting up of limits and regulations that foster creativity. As stated by Cassim Shepard, "the conception of the urban environment [is] a product of creative chaos of

"Scenes": design research seminar for the M. Sc. Architecture and Urban Design programme at Leibniz University Hannover, directed by Riccarda Cappeller
"Scenes" looked at specific *campi*—public squares—in Venice, that were set as stages. The aim was to actively explore through films the creative potential of the tension between material space, perception, movement, and action. The film format of the visual essay was introduced to explicitly display the process of thinking-making as a designerly way of doing, working with analytical and imaginary approaches and testing and experimenting visual and verbal forms of communication. Following Catherine Grant, one of the most distinguished visual essayists and theorists as well as founding author of the Open Access Website "Film Studies for free", the visual essay is a creative research tool that allows people to think in public (2016). It can be used to show the role of space as catalyst, make the constellations and fields of action graspable, and transfer them as narratives. With regard to the design process, the work on visual essays supports the study of juxtapositions, movement through space, and the dimension of time as well as the linkage of theory and praxis through montage, creating a guided narration. Here, selected stories from Italo Calvino's *Invisible Cities* were used as reference and enacted on site. Later, the produced films were taken as departure points to reflect on the question of the Venice Architecture Biennale 2021 "How Will We Live Together?" through critically reorganising and composing the footage.
Screenshots from "Finding Valdrada" by Marie Schwarz and Lennart von Hofe.

DURING A
PROMENADE
WITH
ITALO CALVINO

THAT THE
OTHER
VALDRADA
DOES NOT
REPEAT

AT TIMES THE
MIRROR
INCREASES A
THINGS' VALUE,
AT TIMES
DENIES IT.

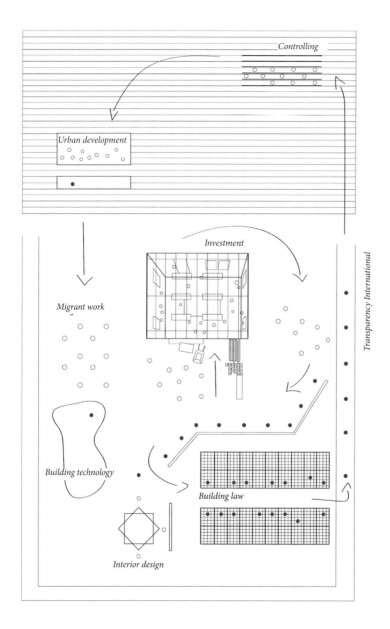

Controlling

Urban development

Investment

Transparency International

Migrant work

Building technology

Building law

Interior design

individual designers, scholars, activists, policy makers, and engaged citizens" (2017, p. 28). He speaks of the "culture of city-making" (ibid., pp. 28–29) instead of urban design, referring to the etymological meaning of culture as a noun of process and action. This means "the constant formation of urban space and society, through a series of overlapping creative acts" (ibid., p. 29), which "involves a making do with materials already at hand, constantly re-using them to create something new" (Cappeller 2021).

Or, as Roberts defines the process of mapping and applying anthropological research methods—which are especially important in the analytical part of design-research process—it is a picking and mixing of methods (Roberts 2018) that—in a wild-thinking manner—mobilises the findings inventively (Latour 2012). This approach is comparable to artistic practices, as discussed with the analysis of the Argentinian artist and storyteller Antonio Bernini in "Urban Bricoleurs" (Cappeller 2021). Looking at the hands-on working process of designers in the context of *Cosmopolitan Habitat* (Schröder, Carta, Scaffidi, Contato 2021) the focus lies on the active creative process rather than on materialising the ideas (see Gänshirt 2007).

The concluding remark is more of a plea: to open research-oriented design to interdisciplinary and more artistic approaches, fostering an inventive agency that evolves throughout the process. As the theoretical reflection for the three research targets—the characterisation of *Circular Narratives*, the thinking-making in design processes and the cultural understanding of space—and the examples have shown, the potential for the creation and transformation of living spaces lies in attentively reading, interpreting, projecting upon, and communicating existing spaces and the circular dynamics of their everyday life.

"Großbaustelle": a documentary theatre play by Rimini Protokoll
"Großbaustelle" (Large Construction Site) is about understanding the multiplicity of perspectives and the social, political, and organisational processes in the setting of a classical construction site. Entering a staged scenery, visitors become observers and active participants who in various sequences of time wander through different stations of a hidden picture puzzle. Given no information, they start at one of the multiple stations and learn by participating and listening to the actors, who are experts of everyday professions, reporting their experience and talking from their expertise in the real working world: the regulations and actions of a fire inspector and a lawyer, the research focus of a professor, the thinking of investors, and the dilemma of journalists who are caught up in the action but whose hands are literally tied. The strength of this narrative lies in the continuous changes of perspective that each time add on to the already known and adapts the whole picture, slowly entering the complex networks and relations that come together in the design and construction of cities, their political and social systems and networks, as well as in active knowledge-creation processes.
"Großbaustelle"—Graphic by Riccarda Cappeller.

Bibliography:

Allen S., Agrest D. (2000) *Practice: Architecture, Technique and Representation. Essays. Critical Voices in Art, Theory and Culture*. Amsterdam, G+B Arts International.

Amin A., Nigel T. (2002) *Cities: Reimagining the Urban*. Oxford, Blackwell Publishing, pp. 1–30.

Barthes R. (1986) "Semiology and the Urban". In: Gottdiener M., Lagopoulos A., eds. (1986) *The City and the Sign: An Introduction to Urban Semiotics*. New York, Columbia University Press, pp. 87–98. DOI: http://doi.org/10.7312/gott93206-005.

Baudrillard J. (1999) *Architektur: Wahrheit oder Radikalität*. Graz, Droschel.

Benjamin W. (1963) *Städtebilder*. Frankfurt am Main, Suhrkamp.

Bond S., Thompson-Fawcett M. (2008) "Multiplicities, Interwoven Threads, Holistic Paths: The Phronetic Long-Haul Approach". In: Paul M. J., Thompson S., Tonts M., eds. (2008) *Qualitative Urban Analysis: An International Perspective*. Amsterdam, Elsevier.

Cappeller R. (2020) "Cooperative Architecture. Urban Space as Medium and Tool to share Narratives". In: *FAM Magazine* 52–53, pp. 142–147.

Cappeller R. (2021) "Urban Bricoleurs". In: Schröder J., Carta M., Scaffidi F., Contato A., eds. (2021) *Cosmopolitan Habitat. A research agenda for urban resilience*. Berlin, JOVIS, pp. 154–159.

Cross N. (2006) *Designerly Ways of Knowing*. London, Springer.

Ferretti M. (2018) "Narrative: Stories from the periphery". In: Schröder J., Carta M., Ferretti M., Lino B., eds. (2018) *Dynamics of Periphery. Atlas of Emerging Creative and Resilient Habitats*. Berlin, JOVIS, pp. 104–108.

Finkenberger I. M., Baumeister E.-M., Koch C., eds. (2019) *Amplifier and Complement. About the Relationship between Urban Planning Artistic Practices and Cultural Institutions*. Berlin, JOVIS.

Gänshirt C. (2007) *Werkzeuge für Ideen. Einführung in das architektonische Entwerfen*. Basel, Birkhäuser.

Giseke U., Löw M., Million A., Misselwitz P., Stollmann J. (2021) *Urban Design Methods. Integrated Urban Research Tools*. Berlin, JOVIS.

Grant C. (2016) "The Audiovisual Essay as Performative Research". In: *NECSUS. European Journal of Media Studies*, 5(2016), Nr. 2, pp. 255–265. DOI: http://doi.org/10.25969/MEDIAREP/3370.

Lang A. (2019) "Pedagogical Tools for Civic Practice". In: Dood M. (2019) *Spatial Practices*. New York, Routledge, pp. 227–36. DOI: http://doi.org/10.4324/9781351140041-23.

Latour B. (2012) "Visualisation and Cognition: Drawing Things Together." In: *Avant: Trends in Interdisciplinary Studies* 3 (T), pp. 207–260.

Lury C., Wakeford N. (2012) "Introduction: A Perpetual Inventory". In: Lury C., Wakeford N., eds. (2012) *Inventive Methods: The Happening of the Social*. London, Routledge, pp. 1–24.

Perec G. (1974) *Species of Spaces and other pieces*. Munich, Penguin Classics.

Rittel H. W. J. (1992) *Planen, Entwerfen, Design: ausgewählte Schriften zu Theorie und Methodik*. Stuttgart, Kohlhammer.

Roberts L. (2016) "Deep Mapping and Spatial Anthropology". In: *Humanities* 5, 5. DOI: http://doi.org/10.3390/h5010005.

Roberts L. (2018) "Spatial Bricolage: The Art of Poetically Making Do". In: *Humanities* 7, no. 2: 43. DOI: http://doi.org/10.3390/h7020043.

Rossi A. (1982) *The Architecture of the City*. Cambridge, MIT Press (orig. 1966).

Schnell A., Sommeregger E., Indrist W., eds. (2016) *Entwerfen Erforschen: Der 'Performative Turn' im Architekturstudium*. Berlin, Birkhäuser.

Schön D. (1983) *The Reflective Practitioner, How Professionals Think in Action*. Aldershot, Ashgate Publishing.

Schregenberger T., Lichtenstein C. (2001) *As Found. The Discovery of the Ordinary*. Baden, Lars Müller.

Schröder J. (2022) "Territorialising Resilience: Innovation Processes for Circular Dynamics". In: Carta M., Perbellini M. R., Lara-Hernandez J. A., eds. (2021) *Resilient Communities and the Peccioli Charter*. Cham, Springer. DOI: https://doi.org/10.1007/978-3-030-85847-6_9.

Schröder J. (2021) "Cosmopolitan Design". In: Schröder J., Carta M., Scaffidi F., Contato A., eds. (2021) *Cosmopolitan Habitat*. Berlin, JOVIS, pp. 12–26.

Schröder J., Cappeller R., eds. (2020) *Cosmopolitan Habitat: Urban Narratives*. Hannover, Regionales Bauen und Siedlungsplanung, Leibniz Universität Hannover.

Schröder J., Carta M., Scaffidi F. Contato A., eds. (2021) *Cosmopolitan Habitat. A research agenda for urban resilience*. Berlin, JOVIS.

Shepard C., Genevro R. (2017) *Citymakers: the culture and craft of practical urbanism*. New York, The Monacelli Press, in association with the Architectural League of New York.

Simmel G. [1903] "Die Großstädte und das Geistesleben". In: Rammstedt O., ed. (1995) *Georg Simmel: Gesamtausgabe. Band 7: Aufsätze und Abhandlungen. 1901-1908*. Frankfurt am Main, Suhrkamp, pp. 116–131.

Wirth-Nesher H. (1996) *City Codes: Reading the Modern Urban Novel*. Cambridge, Cambridge University Press.

Ward C. (1996) [2002] *Talking to Architects: Ten Lectures by Colin Ward*. Sheffield, Freedom Press.

Wolfrum, S. (2015) *Performative Urbanism*. Berlin, JOVIS.

Zardini, M. (ed.) (2005) *Sense of the City: An Alternate Approach to Urbanism*. Montreal, Canadian Centre for Architecture.

Circular Assets for City and Society

Federica Scaffidi

Over the course of the centuries, cities change, transform and renew, giving rise to new spaces and societies. Many cultures have succeeded one another, cyclically changing people's behaviour, renewing local identities, and transforming spaces such as squares, streets, and architecture (Scaffidi 2021b). According to Jullien (2016) there is no society with an unchanged primordial culture and every society and every culture is transformed by others. This calls for a reflection on the importance of culture in the circular regeneration of cities (Dodd 2020; Cerreta et al. 2021; Schröder 2020 and 2022).

Culture has transformative power and boosts innovation. It creates positive impacts and promotes the development of community spaces and the enhancement of local assets (Clark, Wise 2018). A huge body of literature has focused on the topic of cultural regeneration and the development of new life cycles. According to Bocchi and Marini (2015, p. 16), recycling is not a "mere technical operation of reusing or re-purposing discarded or abandoned materials, but more lustrously as a reinvention of vital meanings, as a reactivation of new life cycles". Recycling represents the transition from a linear economy to a circular economy. Literature widely demonstrates the importance of recycling local assets involving local citizens and other stakeholders (Mangialardo, Micelli 2018; Scaffidi 2019). Indeed, community participation plays a key role in the development of circular cities and societies.

With the term circular assets we focus on common spaces, shared and accessible to everyone. An important component of their success is the ability of the community to collaborate and design the future together (Iaione 2015). Some studies have highlighted the importance of social recycling that aims to create inclusive and more open urban spaces and to transform neglected assets (Scaffidi 2018; Walker et al. 2004). In the last decade, much attention has been paid to the socially and creative recycling of marginalised heritage, such as industrial heritage (Areces 2005; Scaffidi 2021a). Still, there is a scientific gap in relation to how communities can cyclically and

Several studies on socio-cultural regeneration have been developed but there is still a scientific gap in terms of how communities can achieve regeneration in a cyclical and systematic way. The objective of this essay is to analyse the recycling of former industrial sites as assets and to identify common aspects that can contribute to criteria for circular design. For this, two prominent case studies for culture-based recycling, Matadero in Madrid and Cantieri Culturali in Palermo, are analysed with a qualitative research methodology.

systematically recycle spaces through culture. Does a valid model already exist? Do best practices exist? Is it possible to identify common lines between practical examples that can contribute to define the criteria of circular design? The aim of this essay is to explore existing examples of cultural recycling of industrial heritage and to identify common aspects that can contribute to criteria for circular design. Two prominent case studies exemplifying strong culture-based recycling are selected and analysed with a qualitative research methodology, including field research, semi-structured interviews, and a materiality matrix.

Analysis of emblematic examples to recycle assets

Matadero Madrid is the former municipal slaughterhouse of the Spanish capital. Its life cycle began between 1910 and 1925 (Amoroso 2015) and finally ceased in 1996, having undergone a progressive process of transformation since the 1970s. Following the definitive closure of the slaughterhouse, some local associations campaigned to have Matadero reactivated as space for the community rather than being managed by a private entity. Its recycling has given rise to a cultural centre that has changed the urban and social fabric of the neighbourhood. Matadero has become a place of cultural ferment where exhibitions, sharing spaces, cultural events, conferences, and entrepreneurial activities can be enjoyed.

The municipality did not just recycle the asset but developed several urban regeneration plans that resulted in new developments for the area. The Arganzuela district has been the site of major urban transformation projects, including Madrid Rio, a recreational and cultural park in the southern part of the city. Thanks to the action of associations and citizens, the recovery strategy for this space has completely changed direction. In 2005, an amendment to the Plan Especial de Intervención (PEI) was approved, which included the recovery of Matadero within a programme of urban regeneration of the neighbourhood, changing the destiny of this disused area. In fact, the development of this centre was not aimed merely at restoring and recovering the structure, but at fostering entrepreneurial and associative initiatives to create new economies and services for the local community. The development of Matadero has focused on creating a diverse cultural offer and on providing an open space for local and international artists. The participatory character of the intervention is a constant in the process, from the slogan "Abierto por obra" (Open to work; Amoroso 2015) to the choice of promoting discussions through meetings and social networks.

The findings show that the effects of what we can identify as Matadero's character as a circular-design project are visible in the new life cycles based on culture, entrepreneurship, research, and sharing. The literature confirms that Matadero is an important example of innovative recycling of industrial assets and urban regeneration. The interviews reveal peoples' attitudes to experiencing this urban space. It is primarily conceived as a cultural area of Madrid, open and vivid, that offers numerous artistic and cultural initiatives. One inhabitant stated that especially in springtime he attends film festivals there at least once a week, and that a considerable number of people attend these events. Two other inhabitants recounted their experiences in the context of the debates that are organised periodically within Matadero. These moments create a stronger connection with the context and develop future perspectives for this vibrant cultural environment. According to the interviews, while there are some critical issues, such as the marked barriers that surround Matadero and create a separation with the neighbourhood, it is still perceived as a socio-cultural space where many social enterprises and the municipality provide services for the local community. Their aim is to improve the use of the asset and to create new networks between stakeholders. Furthermore, the results show a structural impact on the location that ensures the constant evolution of its life cycle.

Matadero, therefore, can be understood as a circular asset that has a positive impact on the development of this part of Madrid and its society. New life cycles have developed in this disused area of the city, capable of reactivating the asset and the entire urban system. The interest shown by the local community in reactivating Matadero has contributed to making this area a centre of culture with new economic activities, art spaces, and social entrepreneurship.

Cantieri Culturali alla Zisa is a former furniture factory, Officine Ducrot, located in Palermo in Sicily. It is an important cultural space in the city, located adjacent to the Arab-Norman castle of Zisa, and consists of 24 buildings of various sizes, constructed between the end of the nineteenth century and the 1950s (Prescia 2016). Today, it has developed new socio-economic and cultural life cycles. The history of Cantieri Culturali is marked by multiple changes in both management and function. The furniture factory opened in 1896 (Di Natale, Lanzarone 2013). Thanks to Vittorio Ducrot's innovative vision, it was transformed from a centre for the production of stylish furniture into a place of innovation and design experimentation and research (Prescia 2016). After this flourishing period, the factory was used as a site for the production of military airplanes during the Second World War (Di Natale, Lanzarone 2013). The factory's original production activities resumed after the war, only to be finally halted in 1968. The closure led to a gradual process of abandonment, and then a partial demolition of the space in 1962.

The rediscovery of Officine Ducrot can be traced back to the 1990s, when the area was acquired by the City of Palermo and a process of cultural regeneration began. In 2012, the I Cantieri che Vogliamo movement (We Want the Cantieri) promoted the idea of a space of culture for citizens, artists, and associations. During the event "Culture for the Common Good", three days of debates, public assemblies, and artistic performances were organised following a call for tenders to assign the management of the space to private entities. Numerous associations, artists, and citizens participated in this event, demonstrating the local community's interest in the reactivation of the space. Following the event, a "Presidium" was created consisting of several working groups. The aim was to carry out cultural activities, involve citizens, and raise their awareness of local heritage management. Culture and creativity are the main engine of its development.

Currently, Cantieri hosts various cultural initiatives, offering opportunities for cooperation and educational workshops. There is a strong sense of belonging on the part of the workers and those who contribute to making this space an open and safe place. The social enterprises established in the Cantieri Culturali alla Zisa are increasingly initiating collaborative projects and processes that contribute to creating a unique space, with participants no longer feeling like guests but constituting the space themselves. The site hosts various associations, schools, and institutes, such as Cre.Zi.Plus, a social enterprise that promotes the culture of sharing and cooperation. As Davide Leone, one of the founding partners, confirmed in an interview, Cre.Zi.Plus is a space with multiple functions that together guarantee economic self-sufficiency, from co-working to business incubation, from a social kitchen to a leisure area. It is an open community, promoting cultural initiatives and attracting young people for entrepreneurial activities.

The circular regeneration of Cantieri Culturali has thus led to a new use of this abandoned factory, creating a new productivity based on culture, on making community, on weaving relationships and innovation, responding to the needs expressed by the community. This circular-design process has certainly had a positive impact on an urban scale, since the entire local community is familiar with the Cantieri Culturali and benefits from its many functions and activities. This reactivation has had positive implications for the socially marginalised urban context in which Cantieri Culturali is located, bringing the population closer to culture and making people aware of art, music, and movies.

Nonetheless, a number of critical issues arise due to a system that is still not very permeable, in which the boundaries demarcating this cultural space from the rest of the city are clearly and tangibly present. These walls not only separate Cantieri Culturali from the neighbourhood but also from other cultural resources, such as the Zisa Castle. But based on exploratory surveys and interviews, it can be confirmed that despite the physical barriers, this space is considered a meeting place for the local community. People and children use the open spaces of the Cantieri Culturali to play football and other games, or to chat with and meet people.

Therefore, Cantieri Culturali can be understood as a circular asset that has positive implications for the development of this part of the city and which is revitalising this place and its society. The findings show that thanks to the interest of the city government and the local community in reactivating this neglected productive heritage, new businesses and socio-cultural activities have been developed.

Conclusions
The findings show that the recycling of neglected assets creates new values and life cycles for those assets, influencing the creative re-generation of the city and society. From the analyses of Matadero of Madrid and Cantieri Culturali alla Zisa of Palermo it is possible to confirm that there are many common elements in the recycling of these former neglected industrial assets. In both cases the community played an important part in the development of cultural and open spaces, but at the same time, local governments played a key role in the recycling of assets. Both areas are socially marginalised contexts within neglected urban spaces. After the recycling process, both areas achieved a better urban quality, especially in the case of Madrid. In Palermo, society has been positively affected by the recycling of this neglected heritage because spaces could be opened up that bring the people closer to art and culture. Furthermore, the spaces of Cantie-ri Culturali are informally used by children and other people in the neighbourhood as public spaces for playing and chatting. The find-ings also show the development of new life-cycles based on culture, entrepreneurship, research, education, and community spaces. The two examples also address the needs of the local community. They recycle a neglected urban asset to create an innovative network be-tween stakeholders and a structural and cyclical impact on the asset as well as on the city and on society. The interviews revealed many topics relevant to the circular regeneration of neglected assets, from cultural resource management to internationalisation.

The materiality matrix (Fig. 1) showcases "materials" (tangible and intangible) through contrasting the two selected examples. It was de-veloped by focusing on the following topics: recycling of neglect-ed heritage, community engagement, actions of the municipality, management of cultural resources, space for everyone, collaborative spaces, socio-cultural activities, social entrepreneurship, new jobs,

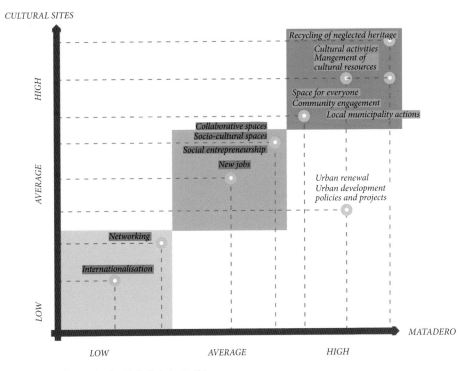

CULTURAL SITES

HIGH

AVERAGE

LOW

Recycling of neglected heritage
Cultural activities
Mangement of
cultural resources
Space for everyone
Community engagement
Local municipality actions
Collaborative spaces
Socio-cultural spaces
Social entrepreneurship
New jobs
Urban renewal
Urban development
policies and projects
Networking
Internationalisation

LOW   AVERAGE   HIGH

MATADERO

Figure 1. Materiality matrix. Graphic by Federica Scaffidi

networking, internationalisation, urban renewal, policies and projects of urban development.

The findings show that recycling neglected heritage is the most important aspect for both examples, followed by the development of cultural activities and the management of cultural resources. High relevance is also given to the actions developed by municipalities to support the recycling of these spaces because they created the basis for activating the socio-cultural recycling of the asset. The development of spaces for everyone and community engagement are also recognised as highly important for both examples. On an average level, the importance of the development of socio-cultural spaces and social entrepreneurship is evident. As a consequence of local entrepreneurship, new jobs have been developed. This has a strong impact on the local community and the spatial development of the two cities. Networking and internationalisation are shown at a low level; they always play an important role in the circular development of the companies but are less important for both examples than the other themes. Collaborative spaces are a very significant aspect for Cantieri Culturali and of average importance for Matadero. Vice versa, urban renewal and projects and policies of urban development are very important for Matadero and of average importance for Cantieri Culturali.

According to this analysis it can be argued that a circular-design approach is characterised by cyclical components that promote the recycling of neglected assets and the social involvement of citizens and other stakeholders. This plays a key role in pushing this transformation, together with the municipality, which create the basis for the physical transformation of spaces. Another important aspect is the management of these resources and the development of new cultural offers. Furthermore, the circular design of assets is cyclical and systematic thanks to the introduction of new forms of entrepreneurship and social enterprises. The latter promote innovative businesses that aim to create social benefits and community spaces. This is extended to other stakeholders. The circular design of assets promotes national and international connections and new networks. The scalar approach of the circular design is not limited to the local assets, but has regional implications in cities and societies.

Therefore, it is possible to confirm that the circular design of assets can be characterised by the following criteria (Fig. 2): reycling of neglected heritage, community engagement, action of the municipality, management of cultural resources, cultural activities, social entrepreneurship, networking, policies and projects of urban development. A circular-design approach to assets must recycle—create new life cycles—starting from a neglected heritage as resource. This circular and cyclical transformation is ensured through community engagement, which plays a key role in the process.

Another important stakeholder mentioned in both analysed examples is the municipality; its actions are fundamental to the enhancement and recovery of the asset and the progressive actions of management. The findings show that there are often new forms of entrepreneurship in these spaces that innovate them; social enterprises create new values, social benefits, and new activities. Culture is an important component of the transformation, for example with activities related to theatre, dance, cinema, painting, and many other art forms. The development of new networks is certainly another relevant aspect, as are policies and projects of urban development. The latter assure the transcalarity of the circular-design actions, with implications for the asset but also for the city and society.

In conclusion, a circular-design approach to neglected assets can positively affect the urban neighbourhood and it can achieve cultural, social, economic, and spatial impacts. Moreover, this approach can be extended to other examples, exploring other theories and practices in terms of the recycling of assets. This essay has aimed to provide new insights as a basis for further research in this field.

Bibliography:

Alvarez Areces M. (2005) "Patrimonio industrial y política cultural en el marketing de ciudades y territorios". *Abaco Revista de Cultura y Ciencias Sociales* 44/45, pp. 45–62.

Amoroso S. (2015) "Aperto per Lavori. Rigenerazione urbana e sinergie organizzative: l'esempio del riuso sociale e creativo degli spazi del Matadero di Madrid". In: *Urbanistica Informazioni*, 2015, pp. 3–6.

Bartels K. (2020) "Fitting In: The Double-Sided Work of Intermediating Social Innovation in Local Governance". In: Sullivan H., Dickinson H., eds. (2020) *The Palgrave Handbook of the Public Servant*. London, Palgrave.

Bocchi R., Marini S. (2015) "Re-cycle Italy. Alla ricerca di nuovi cicli di vita per i territori dello scarto e dell'abbandono". In: *Techne*, no. 10, pp. 16–18.

Carta M., Ronsivalle D. (2020) "Neoanthropocene Raising and Protection of Natural and Cultural Heritage: A Case Study in Southern Italy". In: *Sustainability*, 12, pp. 1–16.

Caroli M. (2015) *Modelli ed esperienze di innovazione sociale in Italia*. Milan, Franco Angeli, pp. 41–79.

Cerreta M., Daldanise G., La Rocca L., Panaro S. (2021) "Triggering active communities for cultural creative cities". In: *Sustainability*, 13, 11877.

Clark J., Wise N., eds. (2018) *Urban Community and Participation: Theory, Polic and Practice*. Berlin, Springer.

Di Natale E., Lanzarone F. (2013) "Recupero delle ex Officine Ducrot, oggi Cantieri culturali alla Zisa a Palermo". In: *Rivista del Restauro Architettonico e Urbano*, pp. 1–8.

Dodd M. (2020) *Spatial Practices. Modes of action and engagement with the City*. London, Routledge

Iaione C. (2015) "Cities as a commons". In: Venturi P., Rago S., eds. (2015) *L'economia della Coesione nell'era della vulnerabilità*. Forlì, Aiccon, pp. 112–122.

European Commission (2021) *The New European Bauhaus explained*. Available online at: https://bit.ly/2YLOr7Y (01.07.2022).

Mangialardo A., Micelli E. (2018) "From sources of financial value to commons: Emerging policies for enhancing public real-estate assets in Italy". In: *Papers in Regional Science*, 97 (4).

Marini S. (2014) "Il territorio reale e il territorio dell'architettura". In: Marini S., Santangelo V., eds. (2014) *Re-cycle. Op_Positions I*. Rome, Aracne Editrice, pp. 22–29.

Ostanel E. (2017) *Spazi Fuori dal Comune*. Milan, Franco Angeli.

Prescia R. (2016), "Il patrimonio di archeologia industriale e la sua rigenerazione. Il punto di vista del restauro". In: *Materiali e strutture. Problemi di conservazione*, n. 10, pp. 103–120.

Scaffidi F. (2021a) "Economía circular, inclusión social y patrimonio industrial". In: Álvarez Areces M. (ed.) *Hacia una nueva época para el patrimonio industrial*. Gijón, Editorial CICEES, pp. 569–577.

Scaffidi F. (2021b) "Palermo-Hannover: Urban stories from cosmopolitan people". In: Schröder J., Carta M., Scaffidi F., Contato A., eds. (2021) *Cosmopolitan Habitat. A research agenda for urban resilience*. Berlin, JOVIS, pp. 136–141.

Scaffidi F. (2019) "Soft power in recycling spaces: Exploring spatial impacts of regeneration and youth entrepreneurship in Southern Italy". In: *Local Economy*, vol. 34(7), pp. 632–656.

Scaffidi F. (2018) "Territorial creativity in peripheral context. Urban and regional effects of the re-cycle of Añana saltworks". In: Schröder J, Carta M, Ferretti M, Lino B., eds. (2018) *Dynamics of Periphery. Atlas of Emerging Creative and Resilient Habitats*. Berlin, JOVIS, pp. 282–289.

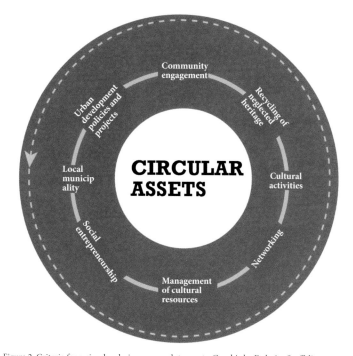

Figure 2. Criteria for a circular-design approach to assets. Graphic by Federica Scaffidi

Schröder J. (2022) "Territorialising Resilience: Innovation Processes for Circular Dynamics". In: Carta M., Perbellini M., Lara-Hernandez J., eds. (2022) *Resilient Communities and the Peccioli Charter*. Cham, Springer, pp. 71–84.

Schröder J. (2020) "Circular Design for the Regenerative City. A Spatial-Digital Paradigm". In: Schröder J., Sommariva E., Sposito S., eds. (2020) *Creative Food Cycles. Book 1*. Hannover, Leibniz Universität Hannover. pp. 16-31.

Schröder J., (2018) "Open Habitat". In Schröder J.,. Carta M., Ferretti M, Lino B., eds. (2018) *Dynamics of Periphery. Atlas of Emerging Creative and Resilient Habitats*. Berlin, JOVIS, pp. 10–29.

Tricarico L., Jones Z. M., Daldanise G. (2020) "Platform Spaces: When culture and the arts intersect territorial development and social innovation, a view from the Italian context". In: *Journal of Urban Affairs*, 2020 1-22.

Walker B., Holling C. S., Carpenter S. R., Kinzig A. (2004) "Resilience, adaptability, and transformability in social-ecological systems". In: *Ecology and Society*, vol.9, n.2.

Culture and Creativity as Drivers for Circular Territories

Alissa Diesch

Since the 1960s, as a reaction to modernist urban transformation projects that in particular promoted car-based urbanisation and related large-scale infrastructures, heritage experts have been increasingly worried about the safeguarding of historic and cultural monuments and urban structures in the historic city centres. The listing of UNESCO World Heritage Sites since 1975 was originally meant to counterbalance these processes and protect historic sites, since in modernist understanding such remnants of the past were often perceived as obstacles on the road to progress. In parallel, from the 1970s, cultural tourism evolved and became an economic factor for places with a long-standing urban history, particularly in Europe. So, beyond the significance of culture for local identity, the leisure industry became the framework for the economic recognition and value creation of cities with heritage sites and cultural institutions. The concept of "cultural industries", related to mostly publicly funded institutions such as historic sites, museums, theatres, concert halls, and libraries, describes the business aspect of these elements.

Towards the turn of the millennium, the growing importance of leisure and tourism and the transformation towards a service and knowledge economy in Europe and North America, step by step, positioned culture as an attractive factor for cities (Richards 2007). A vivid cultural scene offering performing arts, museums, and a diverse gastronomic experience made cities a magnet for enterprises and skilled workers (Scott 1997). Furthermore, cultural events and places such as museums were strategically positioned to stimulate tourism. Culture was now seen as a distinguishing feature for urban and economic development on a global level.

In the meantime, the debate about cultural heritage had proceeded beyond the limits of single monuments to consider more complex constellations such as cities (Choay 2001) and intangible heritage (UNESCO 2003). On the one hand, entire urban structures, settle-

The concepts of culture, creativity, and their relation to the city have been energetically discussed in the last decades. From the declaration of UNESCO World Heritage Sites as representations of past cultural achievements and poles of attraction for tourism to creativity as a means and driver of territorial transformation, shifting paradigms have influenced the debate. As the discussion continues, one possible prospect is the way in which creativity can enhance the implementation of circular concepts in urban planning and governance.

ments, and natural spaces, including their interplay of spatial, social, and economic relations, were recognised as heritage. On the other hand, traditions of performing arts, crafts, local products and services were brought to the fore because industrial production had rendered them precious and individual. Technical innovations did not only replace them but also developed them further, updating century-old disciplines like architecture, arts, crafts, fashion, games and toys, gastronomy, music, performing arts, and publishing. These inventions also broadened the scope with new disciplines like advertising, broadcasting, design, film, software, and video games, for which the term "creative industries" was coined to describe this increasing economic sector.

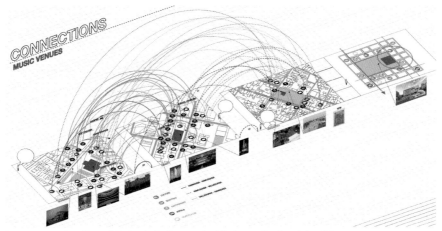

"Connections: Music Venues". Project in the framework of the international workshop "The Future of Creative Cities" organised by Leibniz University Hannover and University del Rosario Bogotá in 2022. The project explores possible transformations and versatile activities of music venues in Hannover (Germany), Vancouver (Canada), and Valledupar (Colombia) by interrelating these places with exchange concepts. Graphic by Nicolas Toro, Karoly Zubek, Martin Trujillo, and Vincent Jeske

These industries now employ more than 7.5% of all employees in the European Union with a tendency towards growth (KMU 2016). The related socio-economic group of producers and consumers described as the "creative class" is a wide cluster of people who "create meaningful new forms" (Florida 2003, p. 8) linked to certain lifestyles and professions. They are highly mobile, looking for places where they find diversity and "the opportunity to validate their identities as creative people" (Florida 2003, p. 9). The creative class also (re-)creates environments that are characterised by the three Ts: technology, talent and tolerance (Florida 2002), highlighting the transformative potential that creative industries have for cities.

Creative industries are considered to be "forerunners in the emerging digital society, in practicing new forms of employment and inventing new business models, in working in networks and co-operations as well as fostering innovation in other (more traditional) sectors" (KMU 2016, p. 53). They are mostly characterised by small enterprises and a very high rate of self-employed and freelance workers (KMU 2016). This is reflected in the businesses' high flexibility and people working in quickly adapting networks, but also in the vulnerability of the sector, especially during crises like the COVID-19 pandemic, when many financial rescue packages did not consider these structures (UNESCO, IBRD 2021).

Through analysing successful creative environments, it becomes clear that a dense and dynamic network of spatially bound and itinerant factors are characteristic. When talking about creative cities, Carta (2007) therefore adds a fourth T: territory, in reference to the spatial relations on which the network is grounded. He stresses local factors such as rooted cultural backgrounds and skills for "producing new creative economies, starting with cultural capital, the highest expression of a location's identity, both tangible and intangible, comprising its cultural heritage, local memory, creative activities, dreams, and aspirations" (Carta 2007, p. 32). The recognition and appreciation of cultural assets—places and people—and their integration into new networks can help to activate the potential of underestimated productive traditions, generating new value-creation loops. Production carried out by people who, due to ethnic or gender discrimination, have been denied access to larger markets can be empowered by integrating them into educational systems or by re-framing their work as design, fashion, or cuisine, as can be seen in the Hangzhou apprenticeship programme (Matovic, Madariaga, San Salvador del Valle 2018) or international design brands such as ames.[1]

The shifting, reciprocal linkages between cultural and creative industries and cities, creating complex and powerful dynamics, are the common denominators that the UNESCO creative city network, founded in 2004, aims to explore (UNESCO 2020). Up to now, only the obvious economic outputs of the growing creative industries for local development have seemed to matter, while further ideas about how to exploit the potential are still to be tested, although the exchange of good practices is promoted (Matovic et al. 2018). Furthermore, the network can help to foster planetary relations, bottom-up globalisation processes, a local-global dialogue (Carta 2007), and support a decolonial cosmopolitanism (Mignolo 2011). The benefits and spill-over effects of cultural and creative industries so far have mainly been linked to metropolitan contexts (Evans 2009, Florida 2003), rural areas have been a blind spot in the discussion (Janc et al. 2020). The extension into a territorial dimension (Schröder 2022) offers the possibility to deepen and extend the potentials of the creative city concept into regional networks. A new mapping and reading of rural areas, particularly in relation to close-by urban centres, can reveal promising new scenarios for creative clusters. In the case studies of Catania, Bari, and Seville (see the chapter "Medways" in this book) and their respective regions, agricultural production and an architectural and gastronomic heritage already form a base for tourism. These site-specific spaces and skills can be enhanced when becoming part of a tighter network, making use of the multi-local and flexible work and life models of the creative class. Digitalisation has boosted spatially and temporally more independent work flows and new individual work and life models, which have enabled international cooperation and networks. Extensively applied and tested during the COVID-19 pandemic, spatially more flexible work modes are now feasible in many working constellations. This paves the road for rural areas as places of residence, work, and the inception of innovative collaborations.

The clustering of traditional craft-based activities and contemporary forms of creative work initiatives can already be found in rural areas (Janc et al. 2020). Through integrating these dynamics into broader spatial strategies and networks the interrelation of resilient communities with territories can be strengthened (Schröder et al. 2019). The food sector is a fruitful example of how rural cultural heritage, eco-friendly mixed cultivation and maintenance of natural spaces can support the right of food sovereignty—a locally and culturally rooted counterproposal to food security— the urban gastronomic scene, and a polycentric urban transformation (Diesch 2020). Seeing examples like this as part of larger networks and flows, "food cycles [can be understood] as a lens and accelerator for urban change" (Schröder 2020, p. 19). The dynamics implicit in a circular understanding of territories increase adaptiveness in the context of resilience (Schröder 2022).

To foster such circular relations and a more resilient coherency within cities and regions, new reciprocal models of planning and governance are needed to establish and uphold these concepts. One possibility to co-produce ideas, implementations, and adaptions are strategic and creative forms of city-making that are to be developed and tested. Creativity can be an instrument and a strategic factor for urban policies and development, "Creative Governance Cities" (Matovic et al. 2018, p. 51) deploy design thinking as a further step to deepen the relation of culture, creativity, and the city. Since 2013, the city of Helsinki has been implementing step-by-step principles of design in the public sector, improving participation and co-creation in "making the city" (City of Helsinki 2018). More creative and flexible governance models and versatile, circular relations between the city and its surrounding territory eventually also create an opportunity to uplift and activate creative potential—both inherited and innovative—in new synergies.

Footnote:

1 http://amesliving.de/ames-world/our-story/ (01.06.2022).

Bibliography:

Carta M. (2007) *Creative City. Dynamics. Innovations. Actions.* Barcelona, List.

Choay F. (2001) *The Invention of the Historic Monument.* New York, Cambridge University Press.

City of Helsinki, Office of Economic Development (2018) *Helsinki UNESCO City of Design. Report 2014–18.* Helsinki, City of Helsinki.

Diesch A. (2020) "Trueque Based Urbanism". In: Schröder J., Sommariva E., Sposito S., eds. (2020) *Creative Food Cycles. Book 1.* Hannover, Leibniz Universität Hannover, pp. 106–15.

Evans G. (2009) "Creative Cities, Creative spaces and urban policy". In: *Urban Studies* 46 5&6, pp. 1003–40.

Florida R. (2002) *The Rise of the Creative Class: and how it's transforming work, leisure, community and everydaylife.* New York, Basic Books.

Florida R. (2003) "Cities and the Creative Class". In: *City and Community* 2(1). pp. 3–19.

Janc K., Raczyk A., Dołzbłasz S. (2020) "Not Only in Cities: Creative activities in rural areas with a case study of Lower Silesia". In: *Quaestiones Geographicae* 39(2). pp. 97–112.

KMU Forschung Austria (2016) *Boosting the competitiveness of cultural and creative industries for growth and jobs.* Brussels, European Commission.

Matovic M., Madariaga A., San Salvador del Valle R. (2018) *Creative Cities: Mapping creativity driven cities. 12 good practices from UNESCO Creative Cities Network.* Bilbao, University of Deusto.

Mignolo W. (2011) *The Darker Side of Western Modernity. Global Futures, Decolonial Options.* Durham, Duke University Press.

Richards G. (2011) "Introduction: Global Trends in Cultural Tourism". In: Richards G., ed. (2011) *Cultural Tourism. Global and Local Perspectives.* London, Routledge, pp. 1–23.

Schröder J. (2020) "Circular Design for the Regenerative City. A Spatial-Digital Paradigm". In: Schröder J., Sommariva E., Sposito S., eds. (2020) *Creative Food Cycles. Book 1.* Hannover, Leibniz Universität Hannover, pp. 16–31.

Schröder J. (2022) "Territorialising Resilience: Innovation Processes for Circular Dynamics". In: Carta M., Perbellini M., Lara-Hernandez J., eds. (2022) *Resilient Communities and the Peccioli Charter.* Cham, Springer, pp. 71–84.

Schröder J., Diesch A., Massari M., Cappeller R. (2019) *City Makers.* Hannover, Regionales Bauen und Siedlungsplanung, Leibniz Universität Hannover.

Scott A. (1997) "The Cultural Economy of Cities". In: *IJURR* 21(2). pp. 323–39.

UNESCO (2003) *Convention for the Safeguarding of the Intangible Cultural Heritage.* Available online at: http://ich.unesco.org/en/convention (01.06.2022).

UNESCO, IBRD (2021) *Cities. Culture. Creativity. Leveraging culture and creativity for sustainable urban development and inclusive growth.* Available online at: http://unesdoc.unesco.org/ark:/48223/pf0000377427 (01.06.2022).

The Atlas as a Project

Alissa Diesch

Cartography is an interdisciplinary project, since geometric, political, and aesthetic challenges need to be tackled. A map, graphically
representing spatial relations, can be described as a "text that simul-
taneously writes and narrates. But […] is not tied to the linearity of
the writing" (Cavalieri 2019, p. 75). Just like in space itself, in two-di-
mensional representation, places and relations exist concurrently and
therefore reading maps is a subjective and creative process, already
implying a project. If the reading has such implications, the making
of maps is even more powerful. Maps have the capacity to "discover
new worlds within past and present ones" (Corner 1999, p. 214); they
are a representation as well as an interpretation of the territory they
depict (Cavalieri 2019). Borges' short story "Del rigor en la ciencia"
(1946),[1] a literary forgery that he attributed to his alias Suárez Miran-
da and the year 1658, describes the necessity to scale and codify a
territory in the map-making process, since a 1:1 representation is too
rigorous and bulky to be usable. The effect of the spatial reduction
(scale) and the abstraction, categorisation, and simplification of the
complex reality (codification) leads to selection, omission, and specialisation.

The consideration of what and how to represent in a map can be understood as an influential act and powerful statement. It gives an interpretation of the represented reality and accordingly never gener-
ates neutral documents, but a project already at this point (Corner
1999; Crampton, Krygier 2005). Critical cartography reflects on the
decisions taken in this process, the mission behind the endeavour
of making a map, and, by proposing a meta-textual reading, understands maps as documents from which these intentions can be deduced. So, for example, a typical world map, a Mercator projection
showing Europe as big and in the centre top edge is not a neutral
depiction of a spherical planet floating in space. It implicitly reflects
a hierarchy and a claim to power expressed by the cartographer in
his maps.

The geometrical dilemma of how to represent a globe in two dimensions turns out to be a rhetorical, even political one, too. No geometrical operation creates a representation that fulfils all requirements

Atlas—the Greek Titan upholding the heavens—is the reference we use for a collection of maps. When consciously focusing on all the decisions taken in the practice and the representations of cartography—the art and science of mapmaking—its heroic and adventurous agency emerges. As a set of maps, an atlas enables transversal readings, the comparison of themes in several scales, and hence the discovery of similarities, analogies, and antitheses (Cavalieri 2019), which make the atlas a creative tool for new projects.

for accurately depicting area, shape and distances—somehow, the orange needs to be sliced, flattened, and recomposed, which consequently distorts relations. The decision about what to put in the centre, whether to give priority to an equal area (e.g. Gall-Peters) or accuracy of shape (e.g. Mercator) projection, or a system of flexible relations, as in the Airocean or Dyamxion maps by Buckminster Fuller, must be consciously taken in all cartographic processes. Thus, Torres García's claim "nuestro norte es el sur"(1941)[2] and his iconic drawing of a map showing South America with the south at the top (América Invertida, 1943) is an aesthetic act of questioning the representation widely perceived as "typical", including its intrinsic hegemonic motive.

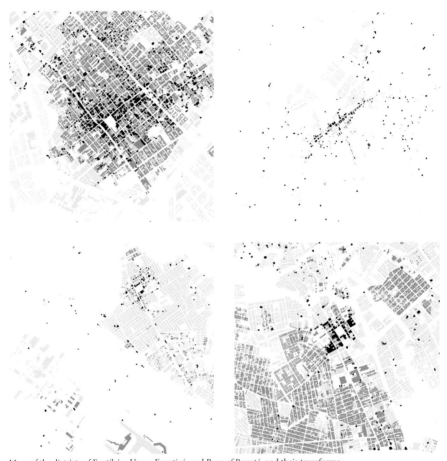

Maps of the districts of Fontibón, Usme, Engativá, and Bosa of Bogotá, and their transformation during the city's conurbation process during the years 1940, 1980, and 2020. The maps reveal settlement patterns of diverse origins like the colonial plaza, dispersed Indigenous structures, informal parcels, and multi-storey residential buildings, as well as their persistence, dominance, overlay, and adaption. Drawings by Alissa Diesch, Giulia Burci, Santiago Guerrero, and Andrea Umaña from Diesch A., ed. (2022) *Atlas Uncovering Territories in Bogotá.* Hannover, Regionales Bauen und Siedlungsplanung, Leibniz Universität Hannover

Pondering the background of the cartographic process, then, reveals the power relations, knowledge, intentions, realities, and hidden purposes of each map and its formation, which go beyond the mere spatial information it provides. This increasingly permeates everyday and professional spheres as technical innovations enable prosumers to create their own specialised and creative maps.

In the sixteenth century, important technological and explorative steps in Europe engendered the need for more maps, especially those representing nautical routes to and territories in the Americas. The Atlantic Ocean—again the reference to the Greek titan—had turned from the edge of Europe to the centre of interest. An atlas "uncovers not only unexpected paths but also unexpected questions [and offers] multiple readings that could empower new histories that are still to be discovered" (Cavalieri 2019, p. 75).

A set of maps showing the same places at different moments in time allows the reading of an urbanistic-architectonical transformation, and through an analysis of the representation mode, the respective contemporary interpretation of these places. Maps of the past hundred years depicting former villages around Bogotá exemplify this idea and show how in the urbanisation process of the territory during the second half of the twentieth century the villages became part of the mega-city. Political deliberations, the eagerness to become a modern metropolis, overstraining in handling an explosive urbanisation rate, means and limits of administrative control, and other challenges can be deduced from this map collection (Diesch 2022). Using this material as a basis to trace and create new graphically uniform maps facilitates coherent readings of the spatial—and related social—transformations. By combining conclusions obtained from the analysis and tracing of these maps with knowledge gained from a set of complementary methodologies, even formally neglected realities could be made visible, representing, for example, Indigenous spatialities in the contemporary city (Diesch 2022). In architecture and urbanism, a creative use of cartographies can enable new visions. A multiscalar approach and architectural understanding of a territory can help to relate places on a larger scale and so provide fresh interpretations and possibilities for transformation. New spatial, social, cultural, and economic relations can be proposed upon mapping territories under novel perspectives and territorial dimensions (Schröder 2022).

The chapters "Mountains" and "Seaside" in this book show the results of design studios that through cartography and the elaboration of atlases articulate fragmented places outside the metropolis anew, creating visions of coherent and resilient territories. The students themselves picked places under the given specific geographical circumstances and elaborated maps in different scales as representations to develop possible scenarios for transformation. The selected territories represent a huge variety of characters and concrete topics; however, in the atlas, common figures can be detected as well as the overarching need for adaptations to new social, economic, and climatic conditions. To tackle this massive transformation when considering large-scale infrastructures, as well as specific places, the concept that "urban and territorial space can be a renewable resource" needs to be built upon (Viganò 2019, p. 123). Each project is an example of how to activate existing places and structures, how to use the performative potential of architecture (Wolfrum, Jansen 2016) and how to link them to larger systems and flows and, in this way, increase the ability of adaptation and resilience. Places can be related to multiple networks in different relations; there are no closed loops, "the system is open" (Viganò 2019, p. 122).

Understanding a design studio as an open platform of mutual learning by exchange is a collaborative endeavour of creating a common project. The atlas as a collection of precise and coherent maps of freely selected samples and carefully elaborated scenarios is a result that permits further interpretations. The iterative approach of combining systematic analysis with inventive imagination, linking implicit and explicit knowledge with creative skills, is one of the characteristics of design. Applying design thinking to conceptual and creative processes (Wolfrum, Jansen 2016) and as a research method (Viganò 2019) broadens the tools of urban and territorial design and the use of a coherent collection of cases. The atlases in this book are to be understood as open systems that systematically show new approaches, relations, and potentials as examples for further reasoning and concrete application. Cartography has shown its agency by unleashing its creative potential.

Footnotes:

1 On exactitude in science.

2 The South is our North.

Bibliography:

Borges J. (1946) "Del rigor en la ciencia". In: Borges J. (1992) *Obras completas 1941–1960*. Barcelona, Circulo de lectores. p. 443.

Cavalieri C. (2019) "Atlas(es) Narratives". In: Cavalieri C., Viganò P., eds. (2019) *The Horizontal Metropolis: A Radical Project*. Zurich, Park Books, pp. 68–77.

Corner J. (1999) "The Agency of Mapping: Speculation, Critique, and Invention" In: Cosgrove D., ed. (1999) *Mappings*. London, Reaktion Books. pp. 213–251.

Crampton J., Krygier J. (2005) "An Introduction to Critical Cartography". In: *ACME: An International E-Journal for Critical Geographies*, 4 (1), pp. 11–33.

Diesch A., ed. (2022) *Atlas Uncovering Territories in Bogotá*. Hannover, Regionales Bauen und Siedlungsplanung, Leibniz Universität Hannover.

Schröder J. (2022) "Territorialising Resilience: Innovation Processes for Circular Dynamics". In: Carta M., Perbellini M., Lara-Hernandez J., eds. (2022) *Resilient Communities and the Peccioli Charter*. Cham, Springer, pp. 71–84.

Torres García, J. (1941) *Universalismo Constructivo*. Buenos Aires, Poseidón.

Viganò P. (2019) "Projects: Urbanism as a Research Tool". In: Cavalieri C., Viganò P., eds. (2019) *The Horizontal Metropolis: A Radical Project*. Zurich, Park Books, pp. 120–29.

Wolfrum S., Janson A. (2016) *Architektur der Stadt*. Stuttgart, Krämer.

INTERFACE

Halligen p. 160

North Sea

Baltic Sea

Hanover p. 128

Vechta p. 92

Schön

Minden p. 110

Diemelstadt-Rhoden

Harz

Rödinghausen

Thuringia

English Channel

Eichsfeld p. 84

Celtic Sea

Sarn Valley

Engadin

Leukerbad

Iseo Lake

Sanremo p. 172

Barcelona p. 100

Ligurian Sea

Collserola p. 192

Seville p. 224

Monterrey p. 118

Alboran Sea

Lima

All projects in territorial relation

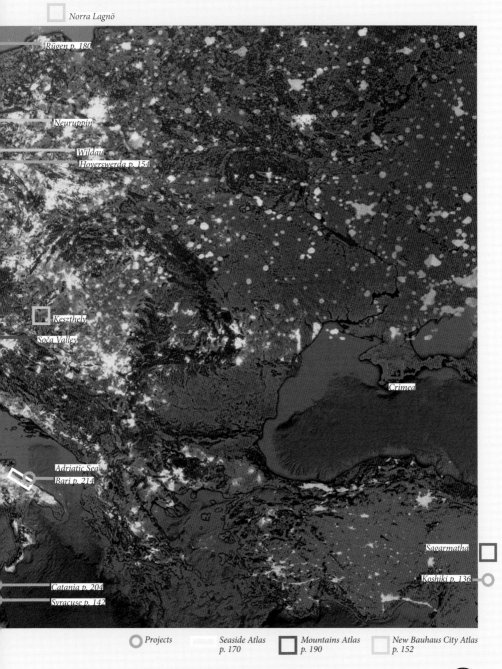

Norra Lagnö

Rügen p. 180

Neuruppin

Wildau
Hoyerswerda p. 154

Keszthely

Soča Valley

Crimea

Adriatic Sea
Bari p. 214

Sagarmatha

Koshiki p. 136

Catania p. 204
Syracuse p. 142

Projects   Seaside Atlas   Mountains Atlas   New Bauhaus City Atlas
            p. 170   p. 190   p. 152

two hundred kilometres

Town networks

Weserhafen/p. 110

Walk the Line/p. 84

Context

This overview of different contextual situations gives more precise information about the territorial relations of the selected study projects. Overall, the focus is on contexts outside of metropolitan cores according to the concept of "Dynamics of Peripheries". What will be presented in all the projects is on the one hand extremes— contexts in which metropolisation/peripherisation trends in the spatial, social, cultural, and economic sense, as well as climate change in terms of water or heat risks have a deep impact—and on the other hand mixtures of intensities and influences. Furthermore, all cases link to ongoing innovation in the specific contexts.

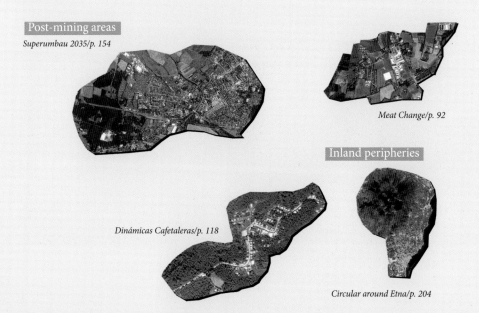

Post-mining areas

Superumbau 2035/p. 154

Meat Change/p. 92

Inland peripheries

Dinámicas Cafetaleras/p. 118

Circular around Etna/p. 204

Welcome to Rügen/p. 180

Riviera dei Fiori/p. 172

Monofunctional touristic areas

Co-Habitat/p. 100

The Guadalquivir Eco-Traveller/p. 224

When Pacman Ate the Motorway/p. 128

Metropolitan extension

Collserola Ring/p. 192

A New Layer for Syracuse/p. 142

The Terra di Bari Experience/p. 214

Land Unter/p. 160

Coast peripheries

Koshiki Dreams/p. 136

Challenges

This evaluation of challenges tackled in the study study projects focuses on spatial issues as concrete expressions of the interaction between larger social, economic, ecological trends within the concrete contexts of the projects. We understand challenges as context-bound and thus dynamic, and therefore their definition is deeply immersed in research into spatial potential and limitations for circular dynamics. What is particularly highlighted is aspects of culture and creativity—fundamental for the cultural shift towards climate neutrality that needs to be based on inclusion, active communities, and better quality of life.

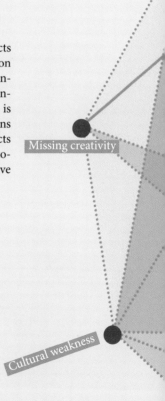

Unsustainable transpor

Missing creativity

Cultural weakness

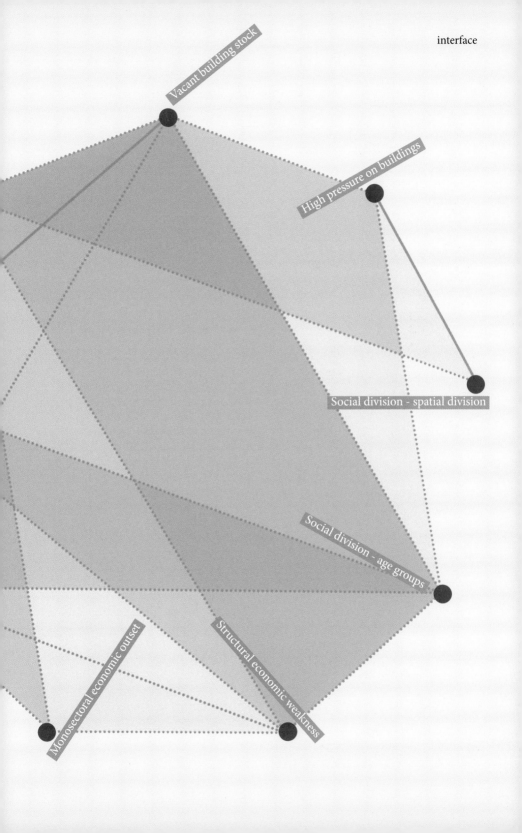

Vacant building stock

High pressure on buildings

Social division - spatial division

Social division - age groups

Monosectoral economic outset

Structural economic weakness

Koshiki Dreams / Satochosato
p. 136

Dinámicas Cafetaleras / Monterrey
p. 118

Situations

The evaluation of concrete situations for the analysis and projection process highlights a considerable range of spatial patterns. Clearly, the impact of urban and metropolitan diffusion—just to state the classic categories of housing, work, transport, and leisure—and even more the tendency to consume space and resources as if there were no tomorrow—can be confirmed in the characteristics and variety of patterns. To construct a taxonomy of situations will be crucial for developing local recycling and transformation strategies, as well as for their up-scaling. Still, the projects will show the high context- and path-dependency of typological elements.

- Town centres
- Agro-industrial building stock
- Rural elements/textures
- Urban elements/textures
- Productive building stock, industrial areas
- Touristic building stock
- Transport infrastructure

Weserhafen / Minden
p. 110

Land Unter / Halligen
p. 160

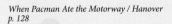

When Pacman Ate the Motorway / Hanover
p. 128

Circular around Etna / Catania
p. 204

Riviera dei Fiori / Sanremo
p. 172

The Terra di Bari Experience / Bari
p. 214

The Guadalquivir Eco-Traveller / Seville
p. 224

Collserola Ring / El Papiol
p. 192

Welcome to Rügen / Dranske
p. 180

Walk the Line / Eichsfeld
p. 84

A New Layer for Syracuse
p. 142

Superumbau 2035 / Hoyerswerda
p. 154

Meat Change / Vechta
p. 92

Co-Habitat / Barcelona
p. 100

Scales

Trans-scalarity is identified as a major factor in the theoretical framework for circular design. The mirroring with the study projects highlights three necessary innovations in terms of crossing the borders of scales: (1) the logics of different approaches and methods in different scales need to be opened up at decisive points for trans-scalar linkages; (2) interdisciplinary linkages within each scale need to be woven into a trans-scalar web of circular design; and (3) the linear approach of former design theory needs to be replaced with fluid, adaptive, and iterative loops of investigation and projection in the process.

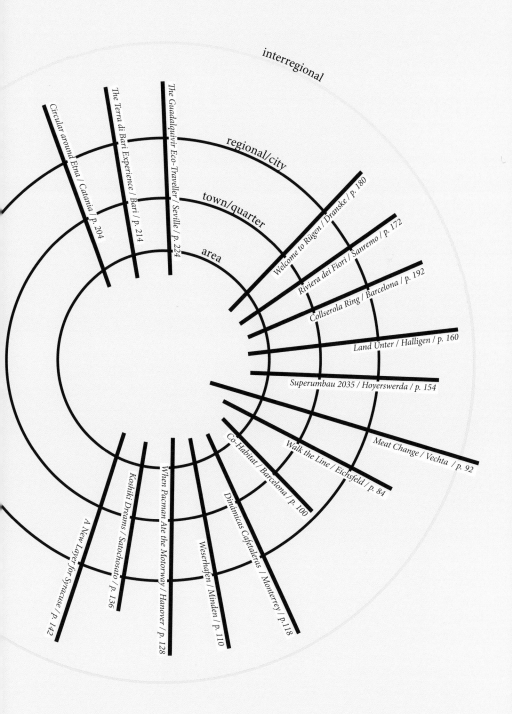

interregional

regional/city

town/quarter

area

Circular around Etna / Catania / p. 204

The Terra di Bari Experience / Bari / p. 214

The Guadalquivir Eco-Traveller / Seville / p. 224

Welcome to Rügen / Dranske / p. 180

Riviera dei Fiori / Sanremo / p. 172

Collserola Ring / Barcelona / p. 192

Land Unter / Halligen / p. 160

Superumbau 2035 / Hoyerswerda / p. 154

Meat Change / Vechta / p. 92

Walk the Line / Eichsfeld / p. 84

Co-Habitat / Barcelona / p. 100

Dinámicas Cafetaleras / Monterrey / p.118

Weserhäfen / Minden / p. 110

When Pacman Ate the Motorway / Hanover / p. 128

Koshiki Dreams / Satochosato / p. 136

A New Layer for Syracuse / p. 142

Strategies

Based on the theoretical framework, circular design needs to go beyond re-use, not only in order to exclude potential unsustainability emerging in complex systems, but mainly to articulate its dynamic vocation. Thus, as a framework for urban and territorial strategies, we understand circular thinking as fundamental to developing active, adaptive, and responsive design processes, oriented towards setting spaces into cycles, starting new cycles, accelerating cycles, and connecting sectoral cycles. What is very well mirrored in the study projects is the multiple dimensions of cycles in this approach, not only material, but also energetic, economic, cultural, knowledge- and value-related factors.

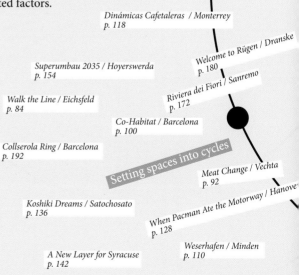

Dinámicas Cafetaleras / Monterrey
p. 118

Welcome to Rügen / Dranske
p. 180

Superumbau 2035 / Hoyerswerda
p. 154

Riviera dei Fiori / Sanremo
p. 172

Walk the Line / Eichsfeld
p. 84

Co-Habitat / Barcelona
p. 100

Collserola Ring / Barcelona
p. 192

Setting spaces into cycles

Meat Change / Vechta
p. 92

Koshiki Dreams / Satochosato
p. 136

When Pacman Ate the Motorway / Hanover
p. 128

A New Layer for Syracuse
p. 142

Weserhafen / Minden
p. 110

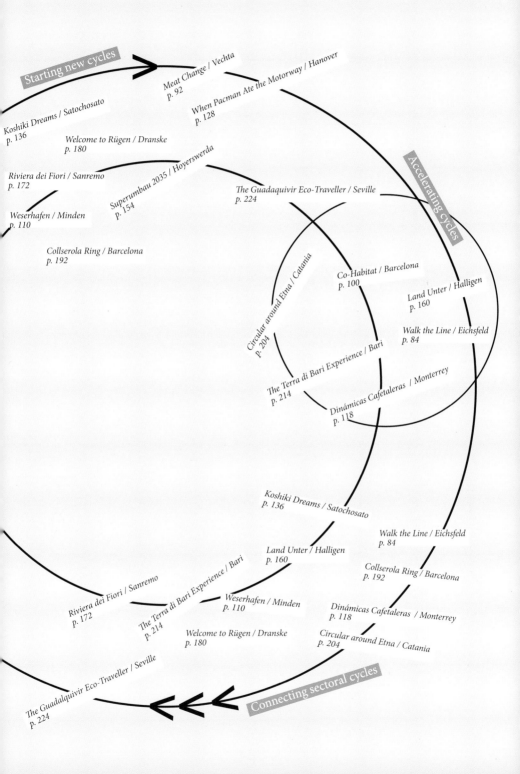

Starting new cycles

Koshiki Dreams / Satochosato
p. 136

Meat Change / Vechta
p. 92

When Pacman Ate the Motorway / Hanover
p. 128

Welcome to Rügen / Dranske
p. 180

Riviera dei Fiori / Sanremo
p. 172

Superumbau 2035 / Hoyerswerda
p. 154

The Guadaquivir Eco-Traveller / Seville
p. 224

Accelerating cycles

Weserhafen / Minden
p. 110

Collserola Ring / Barcelona
p. 192

Circular around Etna / Catania
p. 204

Co-Habitat / Barcelona
p. 100

Land Unter / Halligen
p. 160

Walk the Line / Eichsfeld
p. 84

The Terra di Bari Experience / Bari
p. 214

Dinámicas Cafetaleras / Monterrey
p. 118

Koshiki Dreams / Satochosato
p. 136

Walk the Line / Eichsfeld
p. 84

Land Unter / Halligen
p. 160

Collserola Ring / Barcelona
p. 192

Riviera dei Fiori / Sanremo
p. 172

The Terra di Bari Experience / Bari
p. 214

Weserhafen / Minden
p. 110

Dinámicas Cafetaleras / Monterrey
p. 118

Welcome to Rügen / Dranske
p. 180

Circular around Etna / Catania
p. 204

The Guadalquivir Eco-Traveller / Seville
p. 224

Connecting sectoral cycles

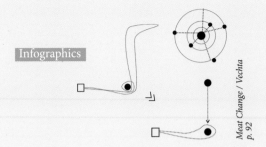

Infographics

Meat Change / Vechta
p. 92

Tools

According to the concept of new narratives in urbanism and territorial innovation, tools need to be invented that deliberately merge analytical and projective traits. There must be a wide openness to inspiration from tools and approaches from architecture, urban design, and urban and territorial planning, combined with graphic design, graphics in other sciences, and arts. Methodological rigour is required to construct design research processes that are able to innovate cognition as well as communication, and that, in particular, can support the interactive flows of project development, strategy building, and policy making, participation and engagement.

Mapping

Riviera dei Fiori / Sanremo
p. 172

The Guadalquivir Eco-Traveller /
Seville, p. 224

Perspectives

Walk the Line / Eichsfeld
p. 84

Co-Habitat / Barcelona
p. 100

Scenarios

When Pacman Ate the Motorway
p. 128

Land Unter / Halligen
p. 160

Meat Change / Vechta
p. 92

Test zooms

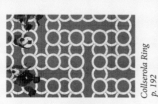

Collserola Ring
p. 192

Superumbau 2035 / Hoyerswerda
p. 154

Modelling

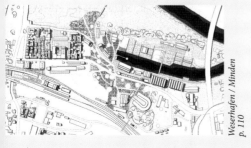

Weserhafen / Minden
p. 110

NEW SYSTEMS

Walk the Line

Rebekka Wandt

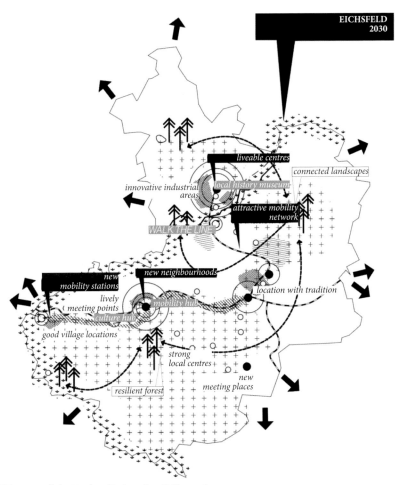

Eichsfeld 2030: Walk the Line from Duderstedt to Heiligenstadt

Texts by Rebekka Wandt and Jörg Schröder

The Iron Curtain was the spatial and structural expression of the division of Europe into east and west, a division overcome a good 30 years ago. This study traces this border in Germany and shows how innovative ideas and integrative visions for the future can inspire the towns and villages along the former border to turn a peripheral situation into an asset through cooperation. For Eichsfeld, a historic region that is today part of Thuringia and Lower Saxony, a possible structural change is defined, focusing on core topics—adequate housing, educational and cultural facilities, tourism, new business models—based on a circular approach for spatial and social densification.

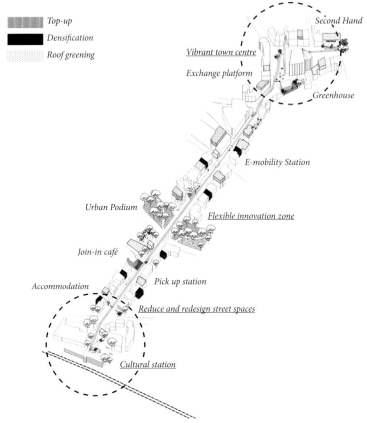

- ▨ Top-up
- ▮ Densification
- ▨ Roof greening

Second Hand

Vibrant town centre

Exchange platform

Greenhouse

E-mobility Station

Urban Podium

Flexible innovation zone

Join-in café

Accommodation

Pick up station

Reduce and redesign street spaces

Cultural station

Duderstadt: Activating the axis from the station to the town centre

The town of Duderstadt in the western part of Eichsfeld is selected as a potential activator for regional cooperation. The project proposes to develop an activation axis from the train station to the town centre. New tools are suggested: vacancy management, interim uses, and innovation zones with showrooms for online commerce, and densification. They contribute to perspectives for the town centre. The axis as a public space highlights a cultural and social dimension of densification and sustainable mobility, with the train station as an intermodal hub linked to the eastern part of Eichsfeld.

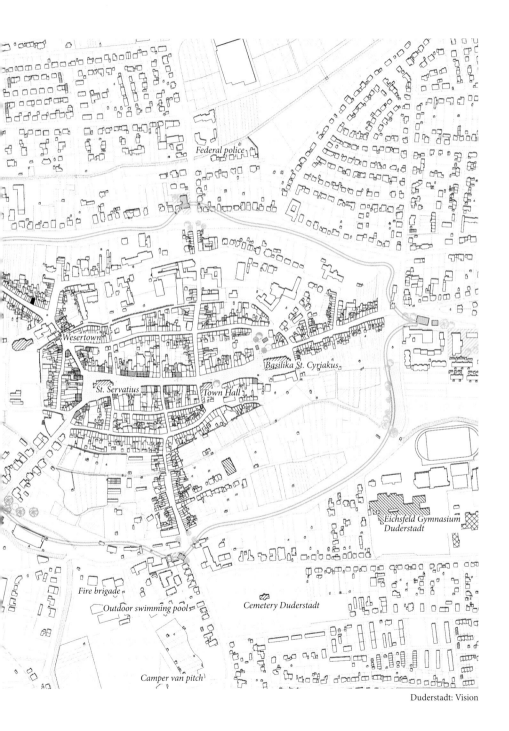

Federal police

Wesertown

Basilika St. Cyriakus

St. Servatius

Town Hall

Eichsfeld Gymnasium
Duderstadt

Fire brigade

Outdoor swimming pool

Cemetery Duderstadt

Camper van pitch

Duderstadt: Vision

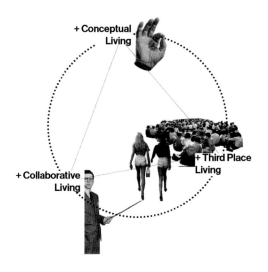

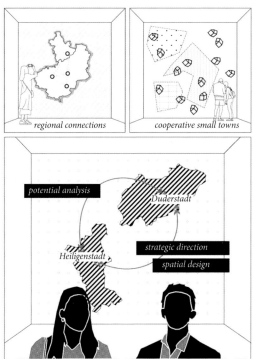

Scheme for a regional cooperation process

How can the qualities of peripheral areas along the border be grasped and innovated? A new basis for action is needed, starting from better networking through digitalisation and mobility. Integrative images of the future can overcome borders and give new impulses for a space of action. Due to the steady ageing of the population, it is necessary to generate a new regional network and cooperation in order to attract young people and to offer an economic, social, and cultural vision. Global challenges and trends, and not least the COVID-19 pandemic, already point to novelties such as digital work and fabrication, neo-ecology, sustainable mobility, and solidarity. Areas such as Eichsfeld—as a mix of rural characteristics with growing towns and a general high urban influence—are facing new demands for involvement, participation, and infrastructural equipment. In addition, there is a need for adequate housing, attractive open spaces, and good educational and cultural facilities. Due to their important role for regional development, towns are at the forefront when it comes to creating a scenario for cooperation towards an attractive, inclusive, and economically innovative region, with higher quality of life and stronger identification by its citizens.

As "cooperative towns", Heilbad Heiligenstadt (with 17,000 inhabitants, in Thuringia) and Duderstadt (with 20,000 inhabitants, in Lower Saxony) can start a regional process that defines innovative goals for development, provides conceptual guidelines, and identifies concrete measures. The study discusses recommendations for action, explains them in more detail, and shows how they are interconnected between different levels of scale.

Core action fields are proposed: reactivation, marketing, and networking, driven by awareness, exchange of competences, implementation of measures, and targeted communication. Only through communication at the political and planning levels, through enterprises, and through citizens can a common awareness of the problems and potentials of the region be achieved. And a change requires participatory and strategically focused planning that is culturally sustainable. The findings of the study can shape the local planning in the region and can thus trigger innovative perspectives.

The Eichsfeld region must meet today's demands for connectivity, climate-neutrality, and a deliberate use of resources, while being neighbourly, supportive, and economically viable. To make the region fit for the future, we need a new set of tools and ways of thinking on different levels. Shaping coexistence to address the question, "How will we live together?" is at the heart of this work. It requires a new acceptance for changing forms of living, and digital and mobile participation, that connect town and country, public spaces as well as culture and tourism as a motor for sustainable urban and regional development. Local identity can only be strengthened through impulses and forms of participation, as well as an active and open approach to cultural heritage. In order to activate and promote existing potential, specific adjustments to formal planning and political tolerance are needed in many places. To achieve common acceptance and to activate people, we need not only the imagination but also the courage to find unconventional solutions and the willingness to work with unplannability.

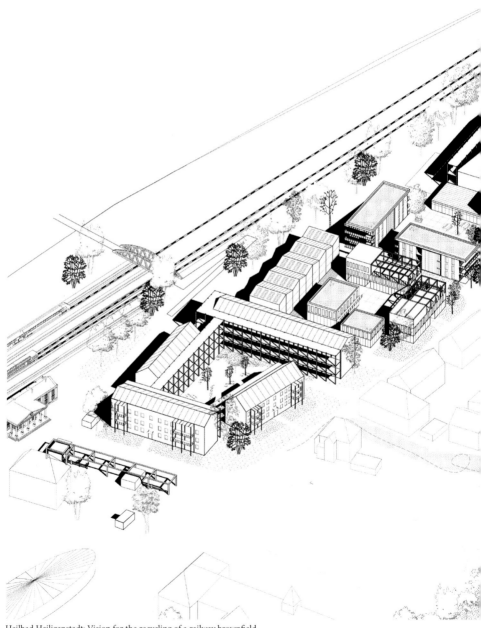

Heilbad Heiligenstadt: Vision for the recycling of a railway brownfield

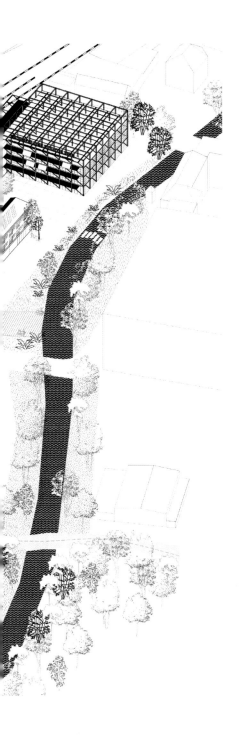

One of the topics for discussion at an "Eichsfeld cooperation table" should be to make the region fit for a sustainable tourism. After all, tourism creates new access to work, culture, housing, and mobility. Improved connectivity based on the train stations as intermodal hubs can be linked to a vision for the town centres as a place of interaction and revitalisation. Duderstadt and Heilbad Heiligenstadt can become new network nodes not only based on regional connectivity but also on targeted local interventions. Thus, the town centres can find a new vocation as trading and exchange spaces with think tanks, new kinds of shops, new living models, and swap meets. In this way, a lively density of cultural venues can be fostered, and the outstanding historic half-timbered buildings of the old towns can be set into new cycles. With the participation of a wide range of stakeholders, new perspectives for the long-term development of the town centres are identified and strategies devised to make the towns fit for the future.

In Heilbad Heiligenstadt, the study proposes densification for empty urban areas and their connection to a multifunctional city centre. Issues of accessibility to public infrastructures and affordable housing should play a primary role and promote a vibrant urban society. In addition to interaction, appropriation, and a new accessibility, social diversity also contributes to the development of a lively town. New connections to the city centre are created, open spaces become a connecting element, and new urban green space is generated. By integrating public functions such as a community centre, a food bank, or various community gardens, new synergies can be created for the neighbourhood.

Meat Change

Julia Theis

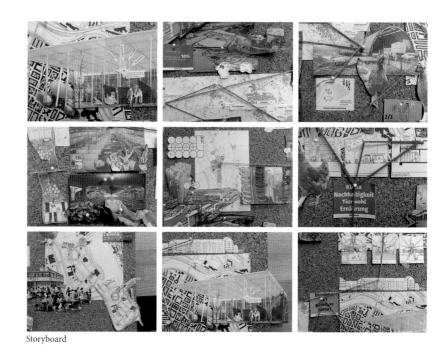

Storyboard

Meat is more

Texts by Julia Theis and Jörg Schröder

Meat Change is a project that understands the importance of a vision for a new food economy as a driver for spatial transformation in urban and rural areas. Currently, Lower Saxony is a global player in the meat industry due to a high number of fattening houses and high export rates. Feed from Brazil arrives at ports and is delivered to industrial stables; animals are transported to slaughterhouses and their meat sent for further processing before being distributed to cities. Oriented towards a more plant-based diet, mindfulness for animals, and new protein sources such as insects, a scenario of a structural change can be developed that offers new qualities for city and countryside.

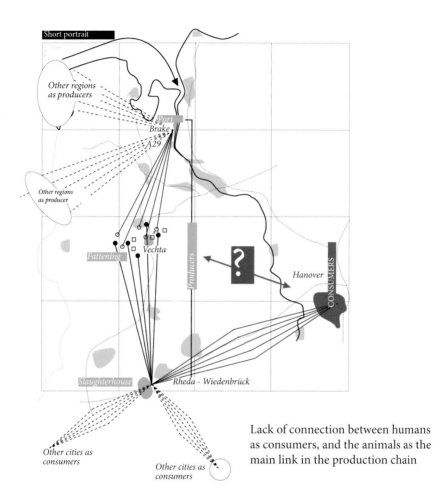

Other regions
as producers

Port
Brake
A29

Other regions
as producer

Fattening

Vechta

Producers

?

Hanover

CONSUMERS

Slaughterhouse   Rheda - Wiedenbrück

Lack of connection between humans
as consumers, and the animals as the
main link in the production chain

Other cities as
consumers

Other cities as
consumers

 Urban-rural exchange

Land modules
● Fattening
□ Supply Fattening: farming
○ Soy Feed
● Veterinarians
□ Free range

Urban modules
■ Consumption, research,
education, culture

Existing and new structures

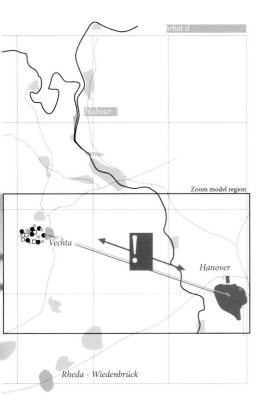

Less meat, more plant-based protein as a strategy to break the vicious circle of the meat industry

Why has meat become a problem? Meat production was initially an agricultural activity, following the principles of a circular economy. With expanding cities, large-scale husbandry, long-distance transport, and the emergence of large-scale slaughterhouses, it has become a mass industry that no longer has anything to do with agriculture. Degrees of processing are increasing, knowledge about the products is decreasing, and the unhealthiness of the products is increasing. Antibiotics and the rapid growth of the animals due to their nutrition, can cause deficiencies and diseases in humans. The consumption of meat is often unconscious or subconscious, since it is included in many products. Today, two out of three young people reject the meat industry and call for a change. What do we eat, what should we eat, and how can we replace meat?

Meat is above all a climate problem. In order to achieve climate goals, we need to cut meat consumption at least in half, due to the high climate impact of meat production in all its steps. Meat is also a global problem that starts with absurdity on an international scale: for example, pesticides are exported from Germany to Brazil to be used for genetically modified soy, which is not allowed in Germany. For the provision of a cultivation area, the Amazon, the largest rainforest and the world's green lung, as well as important savannahs, are cleared. From Brazil, the feed is then transported back to the EU, mainly to Germany and the Netherlands. In the end, we consume five kilograms of plant protein for the production of one kilogram of meat protein and, on top of this, we have travelled twice across the Atlantic Ocean and have massively interfered with the global ecosystem.

Field research: Focus area consumption in urban neighbourhoods, Limmerstrasse Hanover

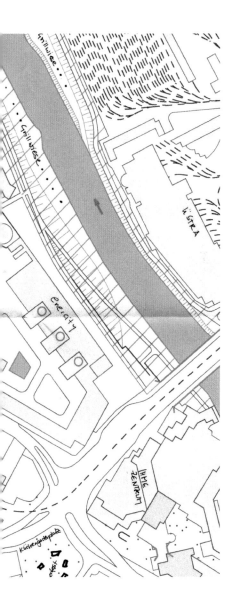

Meat Change places the region of Vechta (as a former fattening stronghold and now a new sustainable production space) and Hanover (as a reconfigured urban consumption space) in a new relationship. In the process, it touches on many topics around the meat industry, on as many layers as possible and with different methodologies. The study builds on intense field research and spatial, social, and economic analysis, in order to propose a vision and development pathway for the model regions, for a change in the meat industry and for the effects of this change in urban and rural space. It is important to look from the perspective of the consumer as well as that of producer in order to create a balance for sustainable long-term development in the meat industry.

Meat Change proposes concrete goals and a catalogue of measures that can be implemented in the logic of city and countryside by public bodies, farmers, enterprises, and citizens on different scales from macro to micro. Goals comprehend a new balance between urban and rural areas, a change in the animal-human relationship, the active participation of consumers, and the economic chances in a new food economy.

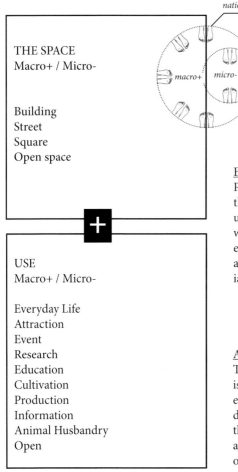

THE SPACE
Macro+ / Micro-

Building
Street
Square
Open space

+

USE
Macro+ / Micro-

Everyday Life
Attraction
Event
Research
Education
Cultivation
Production
Information
Animal Husbandry
Open

Catalogue of measures as urban and rural modules

Everyday Life
Practices of everyday life are defined on the one hand by the fact that they are regular activities (e.g., shopping, going for a walk, doing sports) but also that they are easily accessible in terms of their location and that they are integrated into quotidian flows of movement.

Attraction
The main purpose of attraction modules is to arouse curiosity in passers-by. However, they can mean different things to different actors: e.g., a glass house module that stands on a city square can be used as an attraction for a resident of the district or a tourist (not accessible) and at the same time as an resource for a researcher who works there every day (accessible).

Event
The basic idea of the event module is the same as that of an attraction module: it should arouse curiosity and encourage participation. However, it is temporary and takes place only seasonally or once a year and aims to attract tourists at these times.

Research

Research modules can also be educational modules. However, they have a strong exploratory component. The aim here is to use research to find approaches and solutions for structural change in the Vechta region, for example by looking for solutions for the cultivation of plants in former fattening farms. Networks (e.g. with other universities) play an important role here and should be promoted.

Education

Modules with educational use can be university facilities, schools or training centres. Here, too, use modules can be mixed. For example, a school can also organise an event as part of a funding programme—this would be a usage module with a focus on education/event.

Cultivation

Cultivation plays a key role: it can be found in its original form in Vechta as plant cultivation in the former fattening stables and on fields. In Hanover it is primarily coupled with the use of research. Nevertheless, functions are always connected and networked, even across spatial distance.

Production

Production modules must be functional and equipped with modern facilities. Production modules can also include other uses, for example, by having a welcoming façade or public access. This also makes them an information module.

Information

Information modules can function on their own, but they are usually related to another module, about which they provide facts or data. For example, a micro-information module at a module of animal husbandry (free-range Vechta) can provide information about the way of life of the pigs kept there.

Animal husbandry

Animal husbandry is not possible everywhere. For example, in the city, the only animals that can be cultivated are insects. In the countryside, on the other hand, a large number of free-range animals can be kept. In animal husbandry, animal welfare is paramount. The human-animal space relationship is the focus here.

Open

There can and should also be modules that are not fixed in their use, i.e. open. These modules can be used in different ways by different users.

Co-Habitat

Lucie Paulina Bock

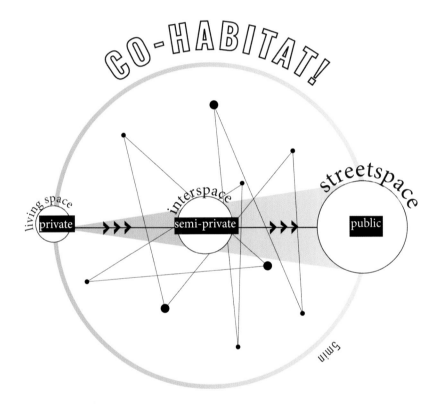

Texts by Lucie-Paulina Bock and Jörg Schröder

Collective spaces for Vila de Grácia are the subject of this study. This urban quarter in Barcelona is severely affected by gentrification and is looking for strategies to sustain the quarter as a social and cultural space. A desire for alternative concepts for living is already expressed in community initiatives, in the occupation of properties, in demonstrations against the tight housing market, and in cultural events. Due to community spirit and openness in everyday life, Vila de Grácia is an ideal place for a study on new collective spaces that can complement the promotion of co-housing in Barcelona and propose new solutions for the challenges of growing metropolitan regions.

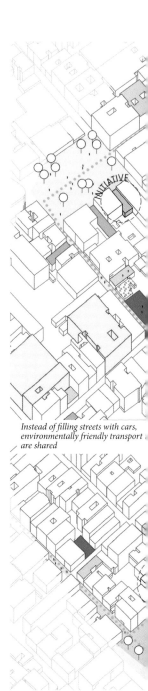

Instead of filling streets with cars, environmentally friendly transport are shared

Vila de Grácia is located in the north of the city centre of Barcelona below Mount Tibidabo. One of the major deficits of this district with the second highest population density in the metropolis is the very low stock of social housing. Vila de Grácia is affected by real-estate speculation and is overrun by tourists. The small-meshed network of 16 squares and the narrow streets are populated by a colourful mix of young professionals, students, artists, and older groups with strong bonds to the quarter. The quarter is characterised by its predominantly low buildings. 94% of the roofs are flat roofs with existing access. Nevertheless, only 34% of these roofs are used.

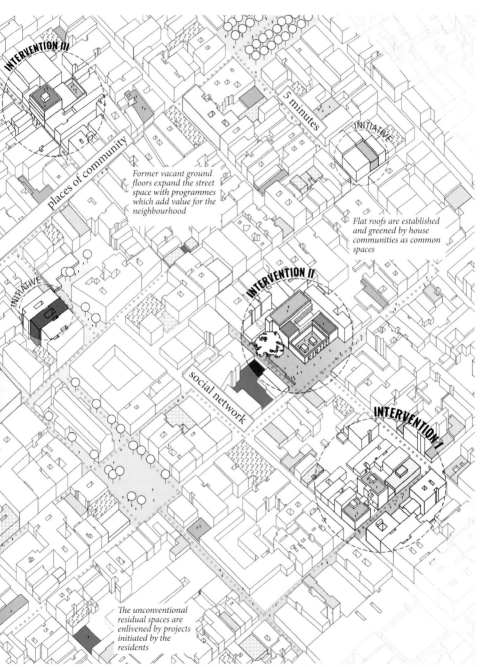

INTERVENTION III

INITIATIVE

5 minutes

places of community

Former vacant ground floors expand the street space with programmes which add value for the neighbourhood

Flat roofs are established and greened by house communities as common spaces

INITIATIVE

INTERVENTION II

social network

INTERVENTION I

The unconventional residual spaces are enlivened by projects initiated by the residents

Overview of collective models in different scales, from houses to streets and neighbourhood

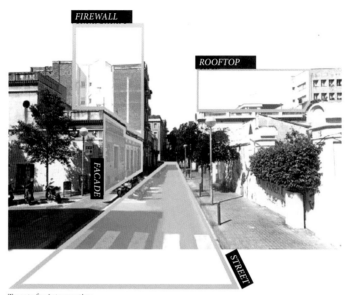

Targets for intervention

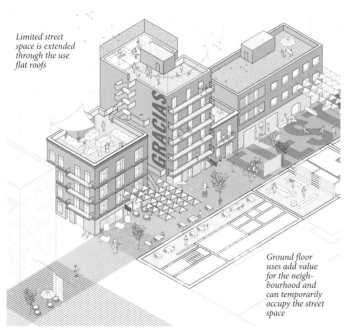

Limited street space is extended through the use flat roofs

Ground floor uses add value for the neigh-bourhood and can temporarily occupy the street space

Activation of streets

Due to its global attractiveness and dynamic economic development, Barcelona has to face the challenges of a growing metropolis. Furthermore, 12 million tourists per year in a city with 1.6 million inhabitants cause high pressure on the housing market, due to Airbnb and similar platforms. High prices for rent become a problem in particular for people with lower incomes, but also increasingly for those with middle incomes. With the economic crisis after 2008, many residents of the city lost their jobs and their homes. During this time, a considerable squatter scene emerged in Barcelona. Activists expressed their displeasure with the housing system by occupying vacant spaces and buildings. As a reaction to this, the city government instituted the Right to Housing Plan in 2016 to increase public housing for rent (although rental properties still make up only 11% of the city's housing), and since 2020 a regulation has made it illegal not to let vacant flats. But there is still a lack of housing concepts that can bring about social change.

The city's housing policy promotes community housing concepts. Such models not only aim for affordability and the economical use of living space, but also for the promotion of collective lifestyles in an overarching sense. They are therefore a response to the increase in social isolation in cities. Such models rely on the overlapping and joint use of space and on the (re)creation of spaces for social encounters on the streets and in the city.

The implementation of collective housing projects is complex because different needs have to be addressed. Concepts such as cooperatives and building groups that aim for common ownership and integrate collective spaces in order to live more cost-effectively have been common

alternatives for several years in major cities such as Zurich. In Barcelona, as in southern Europe in general, such projects have rarely been realised until now. Yet community housing concepts can not only be beneficial for the residents but also improve the atmosphere and liveliness of the neighbourhood and show that the currently dominant model of private use of spaces in the city is by no means without alternatives. The paradigm shift in housing that demands more flexible and adaptable structures can no longer be met by the current predominantly mono-functional concepts.

The attraction of a variety of offers, short distances, and flexibility have led to an increase in densification in the city. This has been accompanied by a commodification of the housing market that leads to speculative vacancies and fragmented neighbourhoods. The privatisation of the city causes the displacement of those on lower incomes and the loss of social ties that are fundamental for a liveable city. Densification has far-reaching ecological and economic consequences with profound social impacts. With this backdrop, the study Co-Habitat proposes new urban elements and networks as catalysts for social interaction. It focuses on the transformation and revitalisation of existing structures instead of building new monofunctional housing developments on the fringes of the city. It also adopts the concept of Net Zero Artificialisation. Different spaces of action are specifically transformed in order to strengthen the urban social fabric.

Co-Habitat aims to answer the question of how Vila de Grácia can be carefully densified and transformed while strengthening co-existence in the neighbourhood. Three selected intervention

STREETSPACE

INTERSPACE

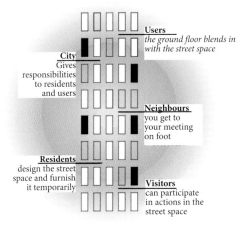

Users
*the ground floor blends in
with the street space*

City
Gives
responsibilities
to residents
and users

Neighbours
you get to
your meeting
on foot

Residents
design the street
space and furnish
it temporarily

Visitors
can participate
in actions in the
street space

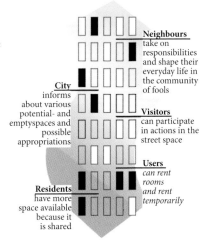

Neighbours
take on
responsibilities
and shape their
everyday life in
the community
of fools

City
informs
about various
potential- and
emptyspaces and
possible
appropriations

Visitors
can participate
in actions in the
street space

Users
*can rent
rooms
and rent
temporarily*

Residents
have more
space available
because it
is shared

Central
everyday life takes place more and
more in the public street space. Private
uses on the ground floor are replaced
by non-profit uses to complement the
street space.

Interplay
the in-between space contains private
as well as communal and public spaces,
which different actors can use according to their ideas.

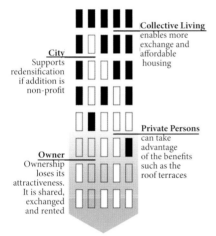

LIVINGSPACE

City
Supports
redensification
if addition is
non-profit

Collective Living
enables more
exchange and
affordable
housing

Private Persons
can take
advantage
of the benefits
such as the
roof terraces

Owner
Ownership
loses its
attractiveness.
It is shared,
exchanged
and rented

Linear
the living space is defragmented
and used less privately and more
communally. Public situations and
moments emerge

models at different scales test forms of community spaces and projects. The specific situation in a selected 500-metre radius (corresponding to the 15-Minute City concept) is taken into account, as are carefully transformed and densified existing structures. For different communities, a diverse range of spaces can be offered to allow for various activities and encounters. Different types of financing and ownership models will be needed that can respond to diverse interests and contexts. The street space (Intervention 1) is put first in the design process in order to loosen the habitual meaning of private space that is anchored in people's minds. Here, public space in particular must take on a new function. The more diverse and flexible the street space, the more likely it is that private space or objects can be dispensed with. Everyday life is increasingly centred on the street space, supported by non-profit uses in the ground floors. In the next step (Intervention 2), a squatted space is programmed and designed to break down the boundaries between public and private and activates the community consciousness of the users. This in-between space is an identity-creating place in the dense fabric of the quarter. The third model (Intervention 3) deals with a very small collective space by transforming and complementing an existing building through community concepts. Together, the different models of *Co-Habitat* meet the need for complexity and diversity in community-oriented living in cities.

NEW PROCESSES

Weserhafen

Mara Piel

Vision: innovation centre at the former harbour basin

Texts by Mara Piel and Jörg Schröder

The former Weser harbour in Minden, close to the city centre and the railway station, offers outstanding potential for the transformation and densification of urban structures. This project claims that recycling the harbour by inventing new productive and space-activating cycles is possible when linked with strategies for a more liveable city centre, the urban riverscape, and new lines and nodes of sustainable mobility. In developing these integrated pathways for a dynamic and adaptive transformation process, a scenario for the Weser harbour needs to be based on new stakeholder constellations and activism.

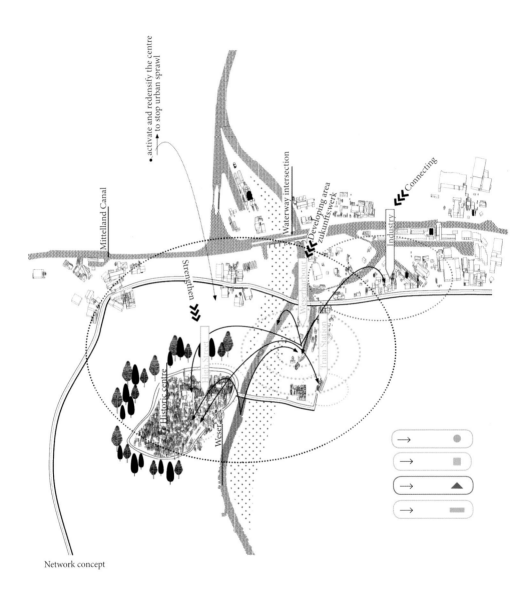

activate and redensify the centre to stop urban sprawl

Mittelland Canal

Waterway intersection

Developing area zukunfts:werk

Connecting

Strengthen

Weserharbour

Industry

High Street

Train Station

Historic centre

Weser

Network concept

Experimental field

As a growing city outside the metropolises, Minden, with its 84,000 inhabitants, is the fourth largest city in the region of East Westphalia-Lippe, an important technology location outside of metropolises in Germany. Despite its proximity to the larger cities outside this region, such as Osnabrück in the west, Hanover in the east, and Bielefeld in the south, Minden is a city with strong regional significance for jobs through a high density of companies. Characteristic sectors are chemical, metal, electronics, paper, ceramics, and wood-processing industries, but also transport and logistics, as well as services, science, research and high-tech. This range of sectors and occupational fields allows 25% of young people to return to Minden after studying or training elsewhere. However, there is a lack of incentives to attract skilled workers to the region.

The Weser, with its important trade connections, has always been central for Minden and the development of the city. The railway station was added as a hub and transhipment point between Cologne and Hanover. Today, container ship traffic flourishes at the East harbour and the industrial harbour, and Minden is a hinterland hub for the large seaports, a function that is planned to be intensified with a new Regioport. A new transhipment centre and commercial area near to the railway station is to exploit the rediscovered importance of the railway for freight and passenger traffic. In this context, the area around the derelict Weser harbour can be further developed. The adjacent urban quarter between the railway station and the Weser has neither changed nor expanded in a century. It comprises the Laxburg workers' quarter, the former station barracks, railway

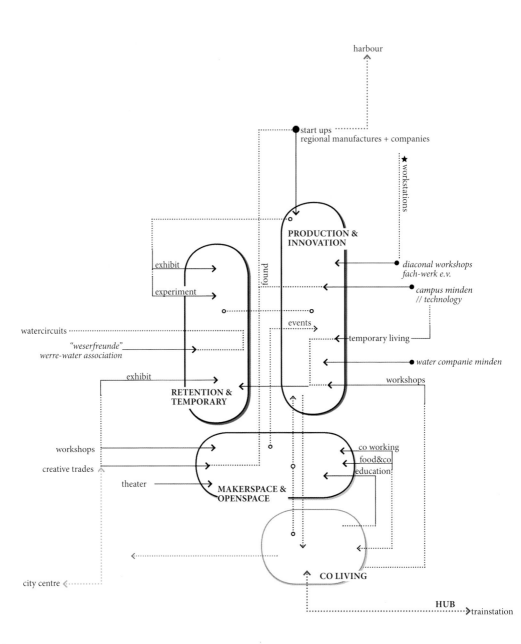

harbour

start ups
regional manufactures + companies

★ workstations

**PRODUCTION &
INNOVATION**

exhibit

experiment

found

diaconal workshops
fach-werk e.v.

campus minden
// technology

watercircuits

events

"weserfreunde"
werre-water association

temporary living

water companie minden

exhibit

**RETENTION &
TEMPORARY**

workshops

workshops

co working

creative trades

food&co

education

theater

**MAKERSPACE &
OPENSPACE**

city centre

CO LIVING

HUB

trainstation

Programming and stakeholder activation

buildings and Fort A, a remnant of the fortifications. This complex and heterogeneous context is a challenge for activating the Weser harbour, with its empty industrial building stock, as a new urban place, and a transformation strategy needs to include a wider radius in order to trigger new dynamics.

The space between the railway station and the Weser can be read today as an undiscovered urban island. It can become a centrally located urban space with the potential to support the positive development of the city centre and of the commercial hub at the station by being discovered, activated, condensed, and reprogrammed. Innovative concepts for the city centre and the sustainable transformation of industry are the basis for activating the island as a new urban place and enabling it to interact with other parts of the city in a dynamic way. Additionally, the Weser river can again become a focus of urban life and a connecting space: new sustainable mobility offers can link the Weser harbour and the railway station to the city centre.

In the industrial sites of Minden, until now, production has been based on materials such as plastics, rubber, iron and aluminium. These industries will be forced out of the market in the fight against climate change. In order to explore and test alternative processes and technologies, as well as cooperation between different industrial sectors, society needs a place to promote this exchange: this can be the role of the recycled Weser harbour.

In order to transform the area into an active urban district that cooperates with the city centre, the station area, and the industry sites, targeted programmatic components are needed—and need to strengthen each other. First, cooperative production and research focused on sustainable resources and production technologies are developed in larger networks, but they need a place to develop and unfold. Products can be distributed from the strategic location at the old Weser harbour via the intermodal transport hub to the whole region in a sustainable and efficient manner. The hub also connects to the large seaports and the metropolises. In the region, peripheral villages and agriculture can benefit from cooperation between production and research and become part of new production cycles. Furthermore, cooperation can extend to other cities in the region. Second, the component of housing corresponds to the desire for a new proximity between living and working and for mixed urban quarters, improving participation and social density as well as strengthening existing housing as well as education and culture. Third, new networks of mobility and mobility spaces contribute to decarbonisation, accessibility, and the presence and visibility of these improvements in urban space. Fourth, open spaces such as the market place or the cultural islands can trigger social interaction if they offer opportunities for free and flexible appropriation. These open spaces are especially important for the socially mixed neighbourhood in the south; they increase the quality of living in the area. The open west side of the Weser harbour is used for natural retention, but temporary appropriation is possible.

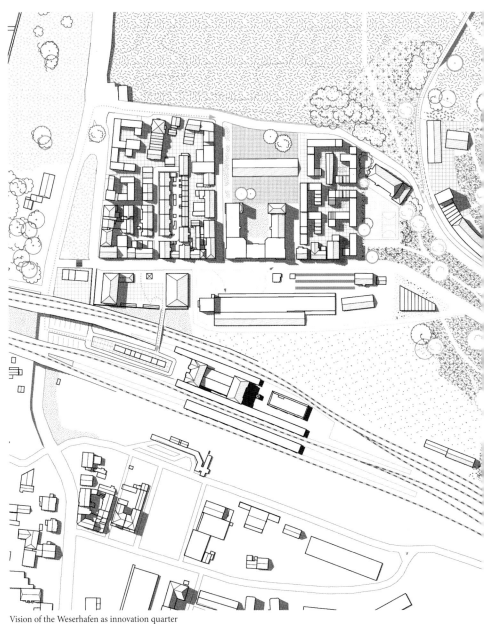

Vision of the Weserhafen as innovation quarter

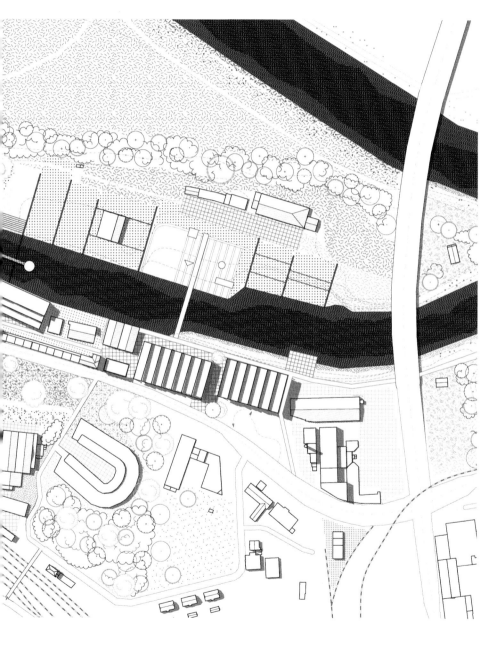

one hundred metres

Dinámicas Cafetaleras

Pia Nicola Kampkötter

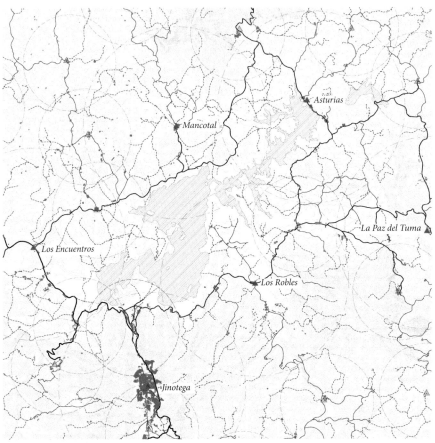

Lago de Apanás and settlement structure

two kilometres

Texts by Pia Nicola Kampkötter and Riccarda Cappeller

Dinámicas Cafeteleras targets sustainable development in Monterrey, a coffee-cultivation village in the north of Nicaragua. The project offers a circular-design approach for the local community and the small cooperatives for coffee production around the reservoir Lago de Apanás. This area near to the city of Jinotega is one of the largest coffee-growing regions in the country. Based on a research trip made in 2019, the existing structures and dynamics that characterise the place are analysed and taken as a starting point for a programmatic design process to upscale existing initiatives in economic, social, cultural, and ecological terms with a circular perspective.

Central concrete square in Monterrey

College of further edu…

Benefic…

Tr…

Roastery

20 km
Jinotega

Processing

40 km
Matagalpa, Sébaco

In Monterrey, with its 468 inhabitants, most of the families grow coffee and many small farmers work together in co-operatives. The central concrete square, built for washing and drying coffee beans in order to enable the local farmers to carry out the production steps by themselves, is the main meeting place for the inhabitants of the village. A local board continues to steer this action, promoting structured and collaborative coffee production that allows the more targeted sale of the coffee, guarantees the quality of coffee for the customer, and stabilises the income of the coffee farmers. Initiatives to form a larger cooperative for joining forces already exist and are the basis for the spatial-programmatic work of this study.

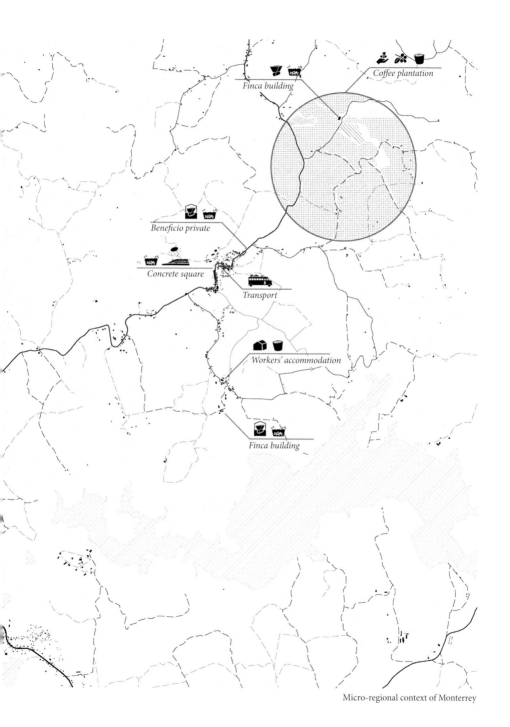

Finca building

Coffee plantation

Beneficio private

Concrete square

Transport

Workers' accommodation

Finca building

Micro-regional context of Monterrey

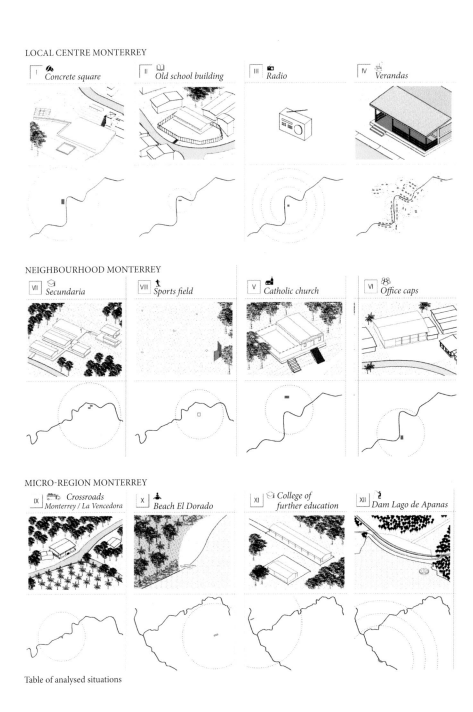

LOCAL CENTRE MONTERREY

I   *Concrete square*

II   *Old school building*

III   *Radio*

IV   *Verandas*

NEIGHBOURHOOD MONTERREY

VII   *Secundaria*

VIII   *Sports field*

V   *Catholic church*

VI   *Office caps*

MICRO-REGION MONTERREY

IX   *Crossroads Monterrey / La Vencedora*

X   *Beach El Dorado*

XI   *College of further education*

XII   *Dam Lago de Apanas*

Table of analysed situations

Site visits and interviews helped to access the local knowledge and to design relevant interventions. Inspired by the collaborative way of thinking in Monterrey, the central idea of the study is to help the local community process and enhance the already existing potential. For this, local places of encounter, education, and mobility are analysed, examining Monterrey on three scales: the village centre, the main village, and the micro-region east of Lago de Apanás. They are connected in order to create a framework and possible sequence of spatial mechanisms for interventions and specific situations. Considering parameters such as public accessibility, local materiality, uses, recognisability, flexibility, participation, and connectivity, this approach includes programmatic, process-related and spatial aspects. The process of transformation in each scale is linked with architectural interventions that support the already existing local use, altering, and extending it. In order to reach sustainability targets, a common new construction system is developed as a modular wood structure. This open system allows spatial openness for specific activities by the local initiatives to take place and to be installed flexibly. Both the plan and execution of the interventions in each of the analysed situations is designed to be created in cooperation with the local community, with professional guidance.

Three exemplary interventions are examined in more detail, in their built realisation and in the accompanying community process. The spatial transformation of the village starts in the centre of Monterrey. Here, the local meetings were previously held in an old storage building. In the project, this building is replaced with an open space for communication that can also be used for other events such as dance performances, theatre, and music. Seating steps provide resting places while market stalls give the possibility for more frequent use. Additionally, an element of Taquezal construction is included. Taquezal is a historic Nicaraguan adobe construction method in which a wooden substructure is filled with a mixture of adobe and straw and plaster.

On the village scale, a spectator stand for the sports field is proposed. The modular system here is supplemented with wooden seating steps where spectators will find a shady and rainproof place to sit. Other elements such as changing rooms and toilets can be added.

The micro-region scale involves the inhabitants of La Vencedora. A small mobility hub is installed at a road junction, with a bus stop and bicycle stands. It includes a collection point for plastic containers, establishing a garbage disposal system and encouraging processes of re-cycling and re-use. The exemplary interventions and the participatory processes for their realisation can be transferred to a larger regional scale.

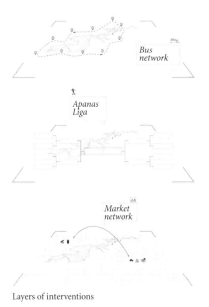

Layers of interventions

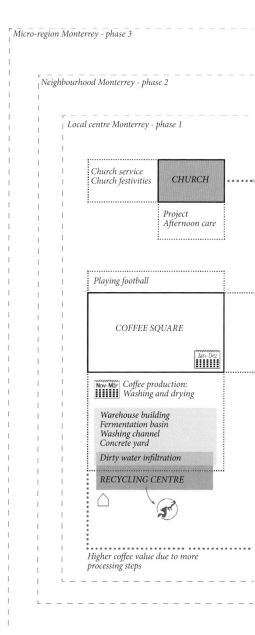

Micro-region Monterrey - phase 3

Neighbourhood Monterrey - phase 2

Local centre Monterrey - phase 1

Church service
Church festivities

CHURCH

Project
Afternoon care

Playing football

COFFEE SQUARE

Jan-Dez

Nov-Mär Coffee production:
Washing and drying

Warehouse building
Fermentation basin
Washing channel
Concrete yard

Dirty water infiltration

RECYCLING CENTRE

Higher coffee value due to more
processing steps

New orientation points can strengthen local networks and regional development. The modular system in wood construction used for the interventions fosters recognition and promotes the formation of a cross-regional identity. For example, a system of bus stops around the Lago de Apanás can improve connectivity. A new market network can foster regional co-operation and the maintenance of local production and sale, supported further by mobile trading points. In terms of recreational activities, exchange among the villages plays a major role and can spread all over the region through baseball and soccer events.

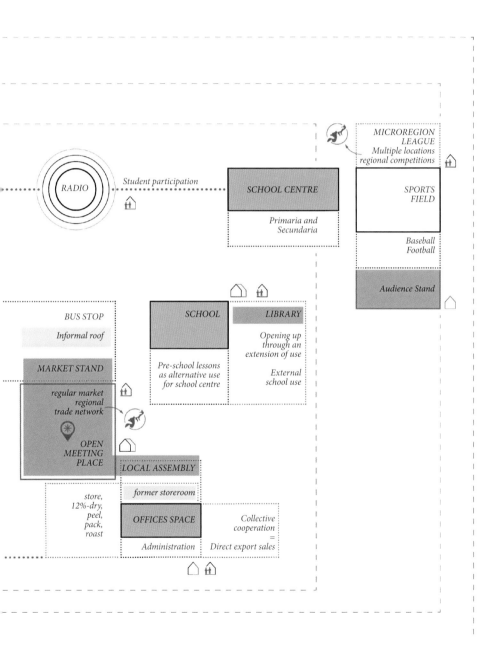

RADIO

Student participation

SCHOOL CENTRE

Primaria and
Secundaria

MICROREGION
LEAGUE
Multiple locations
regional competitions

SPORTS
FIELD

Baseball
Football

Audience Stand

BUS STOP

Informal roof

MARKET STAND

regular market
regional
trade network

OPEN
MEETING
PLACE

SCHOOL

Pre-school lessons
as alternative use
for school centre

LIBRARY

Opening up
through an
extension of use

External
school use

LOCAL ASSEMBLY

former storeroom

OFFICES SPACE

Administration

store,
12%-dry,
peel,
pack,
roast

Collective
cooperation
=
Direct export sales

Scheme of interventions

TRANSFORMATION

When Pacman Ate the Motorway...

Anna Pape and Julia Theis

The motorway as a resource

Texts by Anna Pape, Julia Theis, and Jörg Schröder

Is there a future for the motorway? The idea of speeding along the wide asphalt plain with your favourite song playing on the radio is a thing of the past. Traffic jams and road repairs are the reality. Motorways cut through villages, cities, and nature, dividing them into right and left, top and bottom. Isn't it time to rethink the motorway, to give it back to people? Even to those who experience it from the outside? By adopting the principle of the road construction site, the Pacman Project dissolves the existing patterns and structures and transforms the motorway—as shown in the scenario for the A2— into an open platform, a space for people.

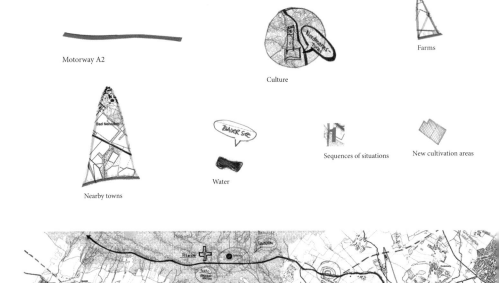

Motorway A2

Culture

Farms

Bad Nenndorf

BLAUER SEE

Sequences of situations

New cultivation areas

Water

Nearby towns

The case study section of the A2 cuts through territories, towns, cities, and nature. The A2 divides into right and left, east and west, up and down. This diagram describes various aspects of how local elements interact (or not) with the A2 and examines cross-connections such as footpaths or cycle paths.

The *Pacman Project* is organised in four steps. First, the systematic approach of the Pacman principle is explained so that it could be applied to any motorway. In the next step, this methodology is tested for applicability. The test case is the A2 from Hanover to the Aue valley. In the third and fourth steps, detailed models are presented and evaluated.

13,000 km of motorways: German motorways are free of level crossings, have separate sides for directional traffic, each with several lanes, and are equipped with special junctions for access and exit. A motorway is a trunk highway that serves the high-speed and long-distance transport of people and freight by motor vehicles. After the National Trunk Highway System (over 130,000 km) of the People's Republic of China, the Interstate Highway System (over 77,000 km) in the US and the motorway system in Spain (17,000 km), the German motorway network is the fourth longest in the world with over 13,000 kilometres (as of 2019).

The vision: What makes the motorway? When it comes to this question, there is a huge gap between expectations and reality. Today, everyone who uses the motorway in Germany is stuck in traffic jams that add up to a total of 35 round-the-world trips over a year, is annoyed by poor road conditions,

Important nodes and crossings

Where are the smallest hamlets?

Local institutions

Focus points

Industries

or is digitally distracted. On top of that, the motorway is a gated community. Why can non-motorists not participate in such a large infrastructure? And is it not quicker to take the train? Not to speak of the ecological impact. *Pacman* is about the question of how the motorway can be attributed to people again in the future.

The Pacman principle: Impulses located at different times and in different places, taking over the highways piece by piece, from the actual state, to short and long impulses, and a new actual state unbound in time.

Where is Pacman? The ghosts are chasing Pacman; Pacman chases the yellow dots on the blue road and occasionally catches a cherry. When you look at an overall stretch of motorway, you ask yourself at which point these particular impulses should be set. The answer: where our guiding goals are most at risk is taken as the starting point for the location of the impulse.

Open the gated community
of the highway

Strengthen linkages in space

Generate spaces of possibilites

Transform linearity

Pacman principles

Sequence models along the A2

Rural and urban scenarios are mixed

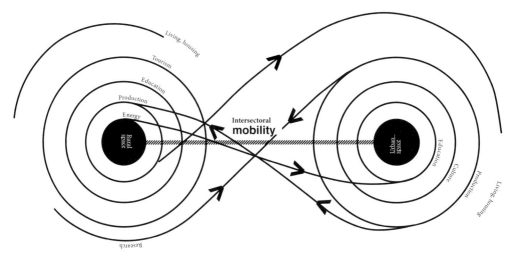

Scheme for intersectoral mobility

motorway = platform

Test model

Adaptation of the construction-site mechanism: Where there are motorways, there are construction sites. This peculiar mechanism closes lanes or diverts the flows of movement. In the *Pacman's* impulses, this mechanism is used and transformed. Since the procedure of partial closure has existed since the invention of the motorway, it is not new and can be capitalised. *Pacman* uses the construction site as a symbol and mechanism to stop, slow down, speed up, or break through the flows on the motorway in different phases.

What can Pacman do? *Pacman* is versatile and should be able to react to different situations and dimensions. Because of this, the principle leaves open the possibility of adaptively generating the individual *Pacman* from a catalogue of sectors, so that a specific spatial and programmatic link with the context can take place. The timing of the complete transformation is determined by the frequency of the *Pacmans*. Thus it is possible to react individually to different dimensions and scenarios.

Mobility change: *Pacman* drives and enhances a rearrangement of the existing logistics and passenger transport system. The rail network will be steadily expanded, along with the launch of the first interventions according to the Pacman principle. This changes the method of travelling and getting around. Travelling by train will be the fastest way from A to B in the future, while the car moves more and more into the background. In addition, *Pacman* is generating new ways of getting around on the linear route, such as new hiking trails or a cruise all the way to Belgium. And it is generating an open platform for new experiences: the motorway becomes a space of possibilities.

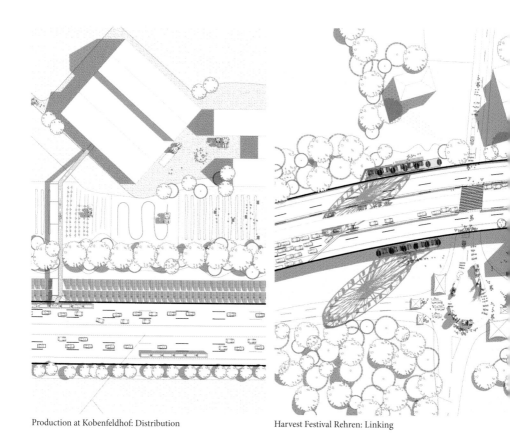

Production at Kobenfeldhof: Distribution

Harvest Festival Rehren: Linking

To test the *Pacman* principle, several *Pacman* scenarios in different situations along the A2 are generated:

Harvest Festival Rehren: Linking
Each morning, a trolley brings all the children from the Aue valley to their primary school. This trolley is a new tool for mobility; until now there has been no public transport available in the Auetal area. In order to bridge the height of the motorway at this point and to make the motorway experience more accessible, the children can complete their journey to school by Ferris wheel. In addition to the construction of a new linear infrastructure, the village of Rehren will be spatially reconnected. A new link is being formed from the centre of the village in the north to the new community centre in the south on the A2. A uniform surface covering and events such as the harvest festival reinforce this connection and provide a new impulse for the village.

Production at Kobenfeldhof: Distribution
The farm typology occurs frequently along the motorway and is usually close to or immediately adjacent to it. This is often seen as a disadvantage, but in this model, it is

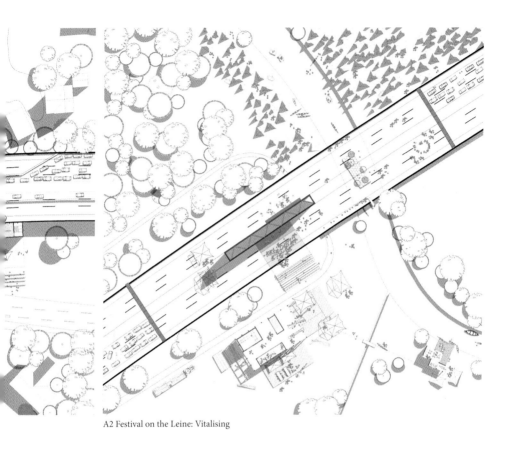

A2 Festival on the Leine: Vitalising

transformed into an asset. The farm is directly linked to the motorway and can take advantage of the new linear infrastructure. Its yields are diverted directly to the trolley and distributed to markets and the city. The farmer uses the hard shoulder for solar-energy production with which he can cultivate his farm.

A2 Festival on the Leine: Vitalising

A new impulse is provided at the interface between the river Leine and the motorway. This activates the surrounding area and creates a new cultural hotspot. A commercial space will be created south of the motorway, where craftsmen, artists, and everyone can work together and exhibit and sell their products. A boat club is also being created south of the riverbank, which will use the water connection to the Steinhuder Meer and Hanover. *Pacman* creates spaces for new cultural activities and brings together the rural and the urban. The stage in the unpaved strip between the lanes on the motorway is used for events and acts as a wooden sculpture on the motorway.

Koshiki Dreams

Lea von Wolfframsdorff

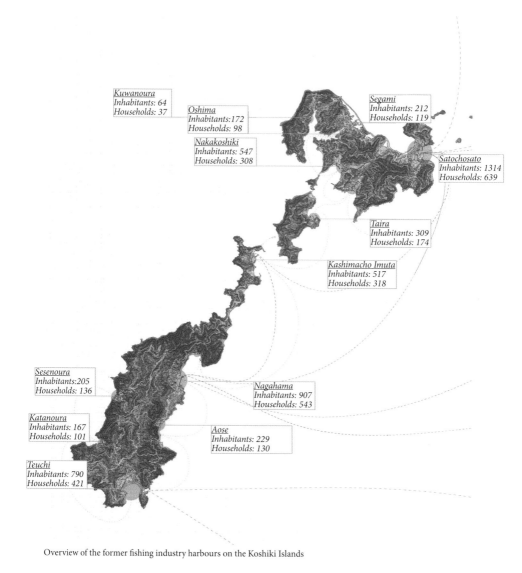

Kuwanoura
Inhabitants: 64
Households: 37

Oshima
Inhabitants:172
Households: 98

Nakakoshiki
Inhabitants: 547
Households: 308

Segami
Inhabitants: 212
Households: 119

Satochosato
Inhabitants: 1314
Households: 639

Taira
Inhabitants: 309
Households: 174

Kashimacho Imuta
Inhabitants: 517
Households: 318

Sesenoura
Inhabitants:205
Households: 136

Nagahama
Inhabitants: 907
Households: 543

Katanoura
Inhabitants: 167
Households: 101

Aose
Inhabitants: 229
Households: 130

Teuchi
Inhabitants: 790
Households: 421

Overview of the former fishing industry harbours on the Koshiki Islands

Texts by Lea von Wolfraumsdorf and Jörg Schröder

The huge harbours of the remote Koshiki Islands in the west of Japan are now empty and derelict spaces—the industrial mass fishing for which they were built is moving further and further into the Pacific due to overfishing. While almost 25,000 people lived on the islands in 1950, today there are only 5,000. Younger people, in particular, continue to move away. Koshiki Dreams sees in these empty harbour basins spaces of possibility that can start an activation of the islands as meaningful and sustainable habitats: they can become focal points of a circular economy, built on the islands' culture, knowledge, natural resources, and creativity.

Traditionally, fish and the sea play an important role in Japan's food supply and as economic factors for its coastal regions and 7,000 islands. In the past, so much fish was caught in Japan that large quantities could be exported abroad. Surrounded by some of the most productive and biodiverse fishing grounds on earth, Japan has developed a rich food culture around fish and seafood. Today, the country is the world's third-largest fish importer, and the empty harbours of the Koshiki Islands are a symbol of the over-exploitation of nature and the consequent breakdown of local economies.

On the Koshiki Islands, as a result of the emigration of young people, the demographic is an ageing population. The main reasons for this pattern of emigration is the lack of jobs and educational opportunities, and scarce connectivity. Thus globalisation, metropolisation, and over-fishing of the seas are impacting on this remote archipelago.

Koshiki Dreams presents a concept for a new activation of the islands, based on their spatial, social, and economic potential. It is a designed utopia that connects the scale levels of the islands, their villages, and architecture. Taking the town and harbour Satochosato on the island of Kamikoshiki-Shima as an example, the concept envisages the occupation of the harbour by a grid with a multiple vocation: as experiential space, as production and research space, as public space, and as infrastructure all in one, contributing to the purification of the sea water. Activities of fishing, farming, producing, living, and visiting the islands are brought into a new circular dynamic that transforms existing buildings, many of which are empty, and attracts neo-islanders to the town.

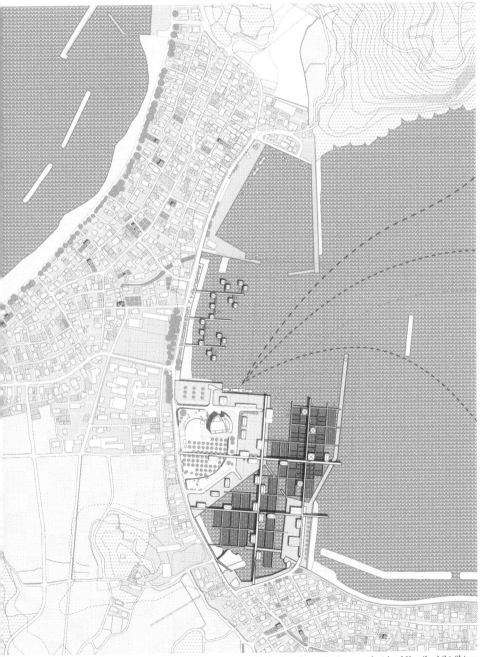

Vision for the Satochosato harbour on the island Kamikoshiki-Shima

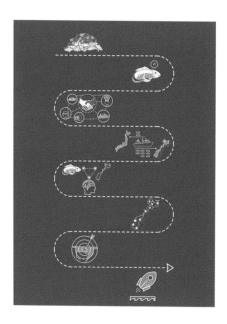

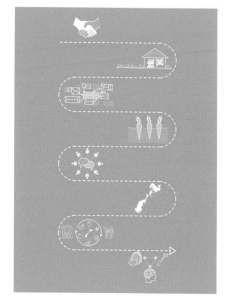

Future fish and sea

1. Developments in the fishing industry mean that island fishing on the Koshiki Archipelago is changing. There are fewer fishermen, boats and fish.
2. In the meantime, the island fishery is focusing on sustainable fishing, lower catches and the marketing of fishery products as sustainable quality products.
3. The fisheries of the Koshiki Islands network in co-operative organisations. In collaboration with local companies, marine products are efficiently marketed on the island, sold to islanders and visitors, and offered in the cities on the mainland.
4. The fish caught around the islands are mainly consumed in the archipelago. Very small quantities are marketed in the wider region. Local distribution reduces transport costs and ensures the freshness of the products.
5. A focus on sustainable fishing and local marketing of fish products creates a regional branding. The Koshiki Islands stand as a brand and place for sustainable fish products of high quality and freshness.
6. Stronger networking of the island locations via the ports promotes exchange within the island community and achieves a higher self-sufficiency rate. As logistical connection points to the Japanese mainland, the ports also offer good conditions for programmatic linkages.
7. The empty harbour areas offer spaces of opportunity in which new businesses or uses can establish themselves. At the same time, the harbours revitalise central locations that are of great importance to the island communities.
8. By converting the industrial heritage of the islands, new economic sectors and links to the mainland can be created without destroying the natural spaces of the archipelago. The ports serve as starting points for the island economy.

Future fruit and vegetables

1. The village community is an attractive aspect for settlement on the Koshiki Islands. It is an important factor for the quality of life of the islanders and a possible incentive to move to the island.
2. Vacant plots of land and houses are made available to the community and renovated and developed in small neighbourhood groups. They provide meeting places, accommodation for visitors, or storage space for community use.
3. Since fruit and vegetables are very expensive on the Koshiki Islands, the islanders are partly self-sufficient with private kitchen gardens. Unused plots of land are planted and cultivated in neighbourhood groups and with new business models.
4. The harvested fruit and vegetables from the neighbourhood fields are used to improve the supply of fresh food for the islanders. Surplus food produced in the kitchen gardens is sold, processed or exchanged on the islands.
5. Working on joint projects and converting vacant spaces strengthens the cohesion of the islanders and their identification with their own place of residence. The resulting common areas offer space for islanders to exchange with each other and with visitors.
6. The products produced in the communal fields can be stored, processed or shipped in the harbours. An exchange of agricultural products with other island locations can ensure a wider range of food options.
7. Growing and selling fruit and vegetables locally increases the islands' self-sufficiency rate. The food is purchased and consumed by islanders and visitors.
8. The Koshiki Islands are gaining prominence through community farming of neighbourhood fields and a high level of self-sufficiency. Products from the Koshiki Islands are associated with craftsmanship, sustainability, and high quality.

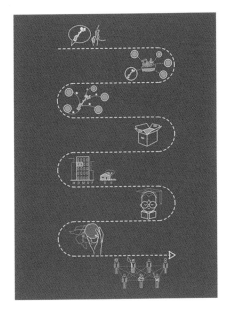

Future living and visiting

1. The Koshiki archipelago is relatively unknown due to the large number of islands in Japan and their remoteness. The two towns with direct ferry connections are too small to act as an urban engine to drive the development of the island chain.
2. Two new ferry services connecting the archipelago with other islands and larger cities in the region will raise the profile of the Koshiki Islands and make it easier to reach them. The possibility of island-hopping will also bring more international visitors to the archipelago.
3. The improvement of the infrastructure leads to new economic relations between the archipelago and the cities in the region. On the Koshiki Islands, offers and uses are created that are connected to companies and institutions on the mainland.
4. With the new connections to the mainland and the changes on the Koshiki Islands, new jobs are being generated. This also encourages former islanders to return to the Koshiki Islands.
5. Mainlanders who want to escape the confines of the city on weekends can enjoy the advantages of rural life on the islands, perhaps buying their own house with a garden there.
6. Through cooperation with the mainland, new training places and educational locations are being created on the islands. For example, cooperation between the University of Nagasaki and the FRA (Fisheries Research Agency) in the port of Satochosato is attracting student scientists.
7. The growing global interest in local and organic agricultural products is attracting more visitors and potential islanders to the Koshiki archipelago. Offerings such as agri-tourism help smallholder farms.
8. The new developments are bringing more people to the Koshiki Islands.

A New Layer for Syracuse

Leandra Leipold

New layer above the Tonnara, view towards the bay of Augusta

Texts by Leandra Leipold and Jörg Schröder

By rediscovering and activating the ruins and the empty buildings of the Tonnara in Syracuse, this study proposes reconnecting the city to the coast in the north. As a space with an open character, the Tonnara can become a platform for culture, education, and research into the interaction of people with the sea in terms of economy, ecology, and migration. It can also play a role in the transformation of the vast oil and petrochemical plants in the bay of Augusta, monumental relics of a present already obsolete due to decarbonisation. The project for the Tonnara explores how new perspectives become concrete, tangible, and experiential through the further use and development of the existing spaces.

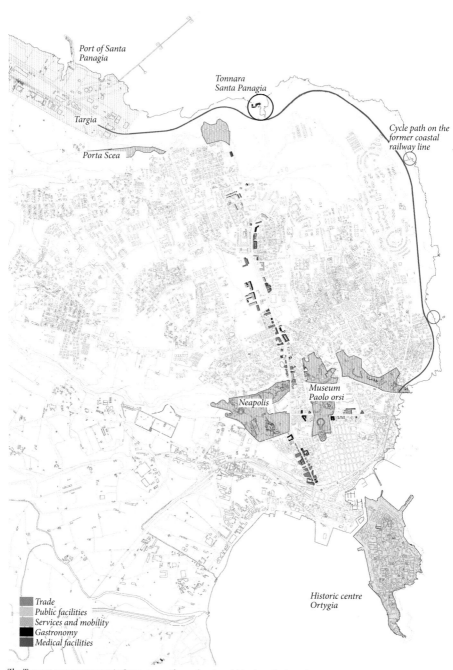

Port of Santa
Panagia

Tonnara
Santa Panagia

Targia

Porta Scea

Cycle path on the
former coastal
railway line

Museum
Paolo orsi

Neapolis

Trade
Public facilities
Services and mobility
Gastronomy
Medical facilities

Historic centre
Ortygia

The Tonnara as new attractor in Syracuse: south-north axis and bicycle path along the coast

New impulse and connection for the city

Repurposing the stock through the new layer

Programmatic and spatial network

The Tonnara of Santa Panagia, situated impressively on a promontory in the north of Syracuse, is inaccessible and a forgotten heritage, characterised by the remnants of small-industrial architecture. It was once an exceptionally multifunctional complex, a factory for the conservation of tuna, a port for tuna fishing, a living place and a cultural location with a chapel for the workers. The buildings' history is strongly intertwined with the urban growth of Syracuse and, despite its exposed peripheral location, the Tonnara was considered an important point of reference for the city and a gateway for networks in the Mediterranean. The area embodies the relationship between people and the sea.

The transformation of the Tonnara of Santa Panagia reconnects the city with the north coast and provides a reference point for the axis of public buildings and public spaces throughout the peninsula and for the new cycle path along the coast. The ruins of the tuna factory are seen as a starting point for the activation; they are not to be reconstructed but supplemented and further developed by a new layer. The resulting multi-layered character and the reinterpretation of the existing structure will open the place up for a new vocation. A number of interventions and the new roof layer unify the area. The roof structure alludes to recent industrial structures in the bay of Augusta and experiments with material recycling. Through its programmatic diversity, the concept is intended to create a lively and significant place that attracts people both temporarily and permanently. Programmatically, the idea picks up on the original urban character and vitality of the Tonnara.

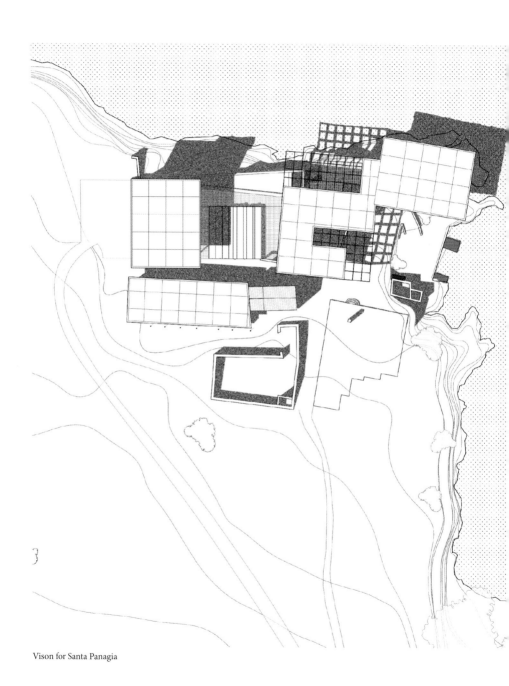

Vison for Santa Panagia

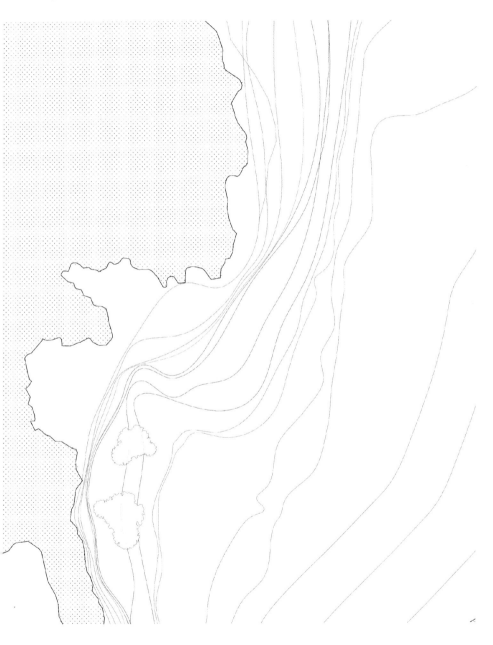

twenty metres

NEW BAUHAUS CITY

Rediscovering Territories

Riccarda Cappeller and Jörg Schröder

New Bauhaus City is inspired by the initiative New European Bauhaus started by the European Commission to enhance creative action and to transform the built environment in order to reach climate-neutrality. The focus on cities set for the course, addresses two crucial dimensions in this context: cities as places where different sectoral changes play together, such as green building, sustainable mobility, circular economy, the use of renewable resources; and cities as spaces to offer new liveability and inclusiveness. Climate change will determine how we understand, feel, and design cities. It is both the stage and a key actor in imagining and realising a resilient way of living and working together. The Territorial Design Studio projects of *New Bauhaus City* (Schröder, Cappeller 2021) respond to this call by setting cities at the core—as places where a multitude of phenomena occur at the same time, where people, space, flows, and ideas interact, where a new quality of life can be imagined and achieved. The specific focus is living places beyond the metropolis (Schröder 2018): this target field corresponds to the 130,000 living places with fewer than 100,000 inhabitants where two out of three Europeans live (Eurostat 2020). Such settlements—medium and small cities, suburbs, towns, villages, hamlets, farmsteads—are neglected in common debates, in media, and architecture. Hence, in this context, "cities" refer to smaller living places and not to the EC-OECD definition of city (Dijkstra, Poelman 2012). In this sense, *New Bauhaus City* aims to add an architectural and urbanistic perspective to research on smaller places (Espon, KU Leuven 2014; Wagner, Growe 2021). Living places beyond the metropolis, their potentials and possible transformation—stressing new connections, enhanced centralities, and new living and working models—are addressed from different perspectives. Some of them face challenges of vacancy, decay, abandonment through work migration, missing potential for a younger generation or a lack of community life, mobility and digital infrastructure.

The theoretical framework refers to research-based design projects and includes creative methodologies not only in the form of projection with case studies (addressing action) but also in the systemic modelling of contextual information and in the formulation of objectives bound to spatial action (Schröder 2021). It offers methodological innovation through design-led analysis and visioning for sustainable urban transformation, highlighting the role of communities for resilience and promoting a new understanding of qualitative density. Starting from a perspective of urban design and architecture, two tools are developed: formats for creative narratives in analysis and project development, and formats for the creative exchange with other disciplines and local stakeholders, opening up new sources of knowledge. The projects merge analytical and synthetic aspects in streams of creative inventiveness, referring to a multi-scalar and interdisciplinary research approach.

For creative exploration, multiple perspectives, and pathways in design research processes, as well as inputs for a theoretical reflection, an active discussion of topics and places was tested in feedback loops. For example, the *New Bauhaus City Dialogues*, organised as an accompanying lecture series for the course, opened discussion in-between theory and practice and expanded the view of urbanism through interdisciplinary perspectives.[1] The series addressed three topics: "New Work" searched for a programmatic and spatial sense of new places, alliances, and environments for productivity; "Experiments" discussed social and cultural initiatives that support the transformation processes of existing urban situations; and "Creativity" examined innovation pathways based on combined imagination and projection processes, including novel and digital means of communication. The dialogues fostered the ability to pose precise questions, increase exchange, and start discussions with experts from other disciplinary backgrounds.

Footnote:

1 The *New Bauhaus City Dialogues* are available online at: http://www.youtube.com/c/FakultätfürArchitekturundLandschaftLUH/videos (01.06.2022).

Bibliography:

Dijkstra L., Poelman H. (2012) *Cities in Europe. The New OECD-EC Definition. Directorate-General for Regional and Urban Policy.* Available online at: http://ec.europa.eu/regional_policy/ sources/docgener/focus/2012_01_city.pdf (01.06.2022).

ESPON, KU Leuven (2014) *ESPON TOWN. Final report 2014.* Available online at: https://www.espon.eu/sites/default/files/attachments/TOWN_Final_Report_061114.pdf (01.06.2022).

Schröder J. (2018) "Open Habitat". In: Schröder J., Carta M., Ferretti M., Lino B., eds. (2018) *Dynamics of Periphery. Atlas of Emerging Creative and Resilient Habitats.* Berlin, JOVIS, pp. 10–29.

Schröder J. (2021) "Cosmopolitan Design". In: Schröder J., Carta M., Scaffidi F., Contato A., eds. (2021) *Cosmopolitan Habitat. A research agenda for urban resilience.* Berlin, JOVIS, pp. 12–16.

Schröder J., Cappeller R., eds. (2021) *New Bauhaus City. Places outside of Metropolis.* Hannover, Regionales Bauen und Siedlungsplanung, Leibniz Universität Hannover.

Wagner M., Growe A. (2021) "Research on Small and Medium-Sized Towns: Framing a New Field of Inquiry". In: *World* 2021, 2, 105–126.

○   Halligen, Wadden Sea
German North Sea Coast

○   Chancay, Lima
Peru

●   Hoyerswerda, Lusatia
Germany

●   Schöningen, Lower Saxony
Germany

⊡   Keszthely, Region Balaton
Hungary

⊡   Norra Lagnö, Stockholm Archipelago
Sweden

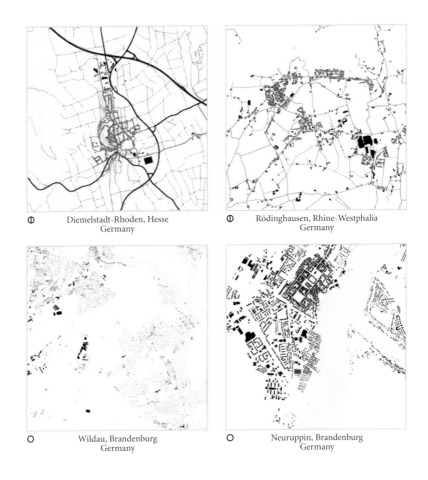

Diemelstadt-Rhoden, Hesse
Germany

Rödinghausen, Rhine-Westphalia
Germany

Wildau, Brandenburg
Germany

Neuruppin, Brandenburg
Germany

metropolitan extensions ○

remote oast area ◔

post-mining regions ●

central germany ①

touristic regions ⦙

one kliometre

Superumbau 2035

Karen Schäfer and Marius Schumann

Storyboard

Texts by Karen Schäfer, Marius Schumann, Federica Scaffidi, and Jörg Schröder

Decarbonisation will cause deep structural change in mining regions. While conflicts surrounding ecological compatibility and the consequences for both people and nature are fuelled by remaining mines (particularly opencast mines) and power plants, coal mining in Germany has already been marked for phase-out by 2038. As desirable as this development is in terms of the ecological crisis, it has challenging consequences for the economy and society in the region. Beyond that, the exit from coal is not sufficient to achieve sustainability. Spatial visions for cities and villages are needed.

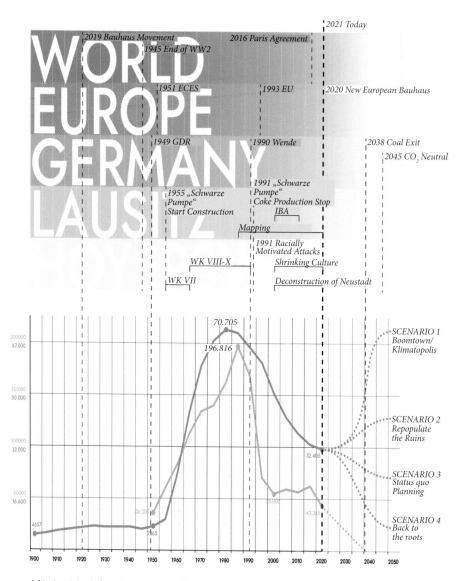

WORLD
EUROPE
GERMANY
LAUSITZ

2021 Today

2019 Bauhaus Movement
1945 End of WW2
2016 Paris Agreement

1951 ECES
1993 EU
2020 New European Bauhaus

1949 GDR
1990 Wende
2038 Coal Exit
2045 CO$_2$ Neutral

1955 „Schwarze Pumpe" Start Construction
1991 „Schwarze Pumpe" Coke Production Stop
IBA

Mapping

1991 Racially Motivated Attacks

WK VIII-X
Shrinking Culture

WK VII
Deconstruction of Neustadt

70.705

196.816

SCENARIO 1
Boomtown/
Klimatopolis

SCENARIO 2
Repopulate
the Ruins

32.405

SCENARIO 3
Status quo
Planning

35.000

43.245

SCENARIO 4
Back to
the roots

26.200

7.465

4.657

200000
67.000

150000
50.000

100000
33.000

50000
16.600

1900 1910 1920 1930 1940 1950 1960 1970 1980 1990 2000 2010 2020 2030 2040 2050

● Lignite mining in Lusatia (in 1000)   ● Population Hoyerswerda

Scenarios / based on: Statistik der Kohlenwirtschaft (Statista, 15. April 21);
Einwohnerentwicklung von Hoyerswerda (Wikipedia)

This project analyses the region of Lusatia as an example of the imminent structural change due to the decision to end the use and the mining of coal in Germany. Substantial funding is foreseen for four post-mining regions in order to cope with this change. Nevertheless, spatial visions for cities and villages and their regional cooperation in this process are missing. *Superumbau* (German for "the great transformation") highlights the potential not only of dismantled industrial sites, power plants, and open mines as resources in a transformation process, but advocates the inclusion of the existing building stock and urban structures too, in an overall recycling approach. Hence, post-mining areas could become model regions for transformation to sustainability based on the recycling of space. Since they are not part of the growing metropolitan agglomerations and already have to cope with structural weakness, a recycling of these resources needs to be based on new cycles of economic and social activities that—and this is the hypothesis of the project—can start from disruptive and experimental visions of how to use the spatial and material resources offered through the exit from coal.

The project claims that the activation of these resources can be linked to new business models and economic perspectives—if it is merged with social innovation, cultural strategies, and spatial renewal. Furthermore, a wider view is essential, able to transform the area at several spatial scales based on an assessment of multiple aspects constituting the territory. In particular, cultural aspects are at the forefront, to support the necessary change to sustainability. In this regard, the logic of recycling can be transformative: it can start and enhance resilient and sustainable territorial innovation (Scaffidi 2019; Schröder 2022).

The Lusatia region is an example of processes of structural change related to the end of mining and the use of coal. In the 2010s, the International Building Exhibition in the region addressed the creation of a lake district by filling former mines with water. Thus, not only a cultural expression of recycling but also the foundation for touristic economy can be achieved. In 2020, Federal and State governments declared Lusatia a target region to support structural change, along with the exit from coal. For example, it is planned to locate large research facilities in the area that deal with climate change and increasingly scarce resources as pressing questions of the future. Public transport infrastructure and resource management are also being improved.

The "Zukunftsfabrik Lausitz" is proposed as an open laboratory for addressing these urgent topics and to attract scientists and start-ups from all over the world. By combining technologies with regional and local potentials and processes, transferable models for other post-mining regions can be expected. Long-term effects for the region would include synergies with industry, tourism, and society. Although substantial investment is foreseen, the creation of resilient spatial frameworks and transformation processes involving existing networks and able to face future changes are not yet in the foreground.

Scaffidi F. (2019) "Soft power in recycling spaces: exploring spatial impacts of regeneration and youth entrepreneurship in Southern Italy". In: *Local Economy*, vol. 34(7), pp. 632–656.

Schröder J. (2022) "Territorialising Resilience: innovation processes for circular dynamics". In: Carta M., Perbellini M., Lara-Hernandez J., eds. (2022) *Resilient Communities and the Peccioli Charter*. Cham, Springer. pp. 71–84.

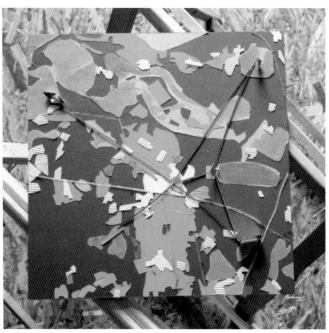

Network mode

Hoyerswerda Neustadt: Urban Hub

FORM
FOLLOWS
~~FUNCTION~~
PLANET

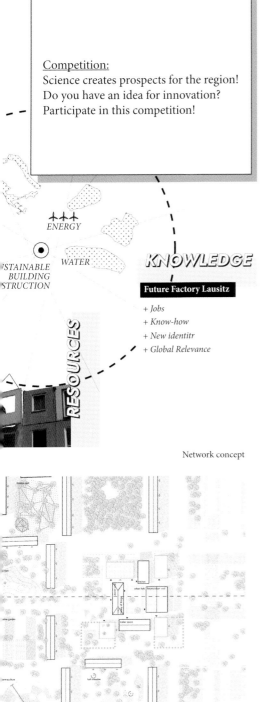

Competition:
Science creates prospects for the region!
Do you have an idea for innovation?
Participate in this competition!

ENERGY

STAINABLE   WATER
BUILDING
STRUCTION

KNOWLEDGE

Future Factory Lausitz

+ Jobs
+ Know-how
+ New identitr
+ Global Relevance

RESOURCES

Network concept

Hoyerswerda Neustadt: New urban density

The project *Superumbau* bases its exploration of Lusatia on the evidence that living places play a major role in the imagination and realisation of a future vision of how we live and work together. The project proposes several new ways of dealing with a process of change through spatial inventiveness, for example in placing a mix of new research facilities, production, and touristic sites at the lakes, creating a new regional network. In this network, a new role for the city of Hoyerswerda could be defined, now a shrinking city with considerable empty building stock, in particular in its new areas. Planned as a model socialist city, a total of ten residential complexes and tens of thousands of apartments were built outside of the centre.

Here, *Superumbau* suggests a twin strategy: on the one hand, to recycle materials from the destroyed buildings for new projects in the region or even for export to growing metropolises such as Berlin, and, on the other hand, to stimulate and support the further use of existing buildings with a vision of a vivid quarter that offers generous space—a resource that is becoming increasingly unaffordable in metropolises. A creative hub called "urban connector" will boost circular economy and business models based on the recycling of materials. It introduces new spatial and social density in the quarter and will attract newcomers. The hub as a space of possibilities and encounter creates new networks and activates existing ones, embodying creative processes to shape the future of the region together.

Land Unter

Kristina Gergert and Pia-Marie Hoff

Collage of a storm flood

Texts by Kristina Gergert, Pia-Maire Hoff, and Riccarda Cappeller

This study offers an alternative perspective on the Wadden Sea, which is conventionally seen only as a natural space between sea and land on the German North Sea coast. Focusing on the Halligen—small protected marsh islands without dikes—the study discovers the Wadden Sea as a cultural space and a human habitat endangered by climate change. Taking care of nature is inscribed in this settlement pattern, which offers both a major resource to increase awareness and an experience of the natural space. Furthermore, the Halligen offer valuable models for dealing with rising sea levels and for adapting human habitats to natural processes through the use of traditional knowledge.

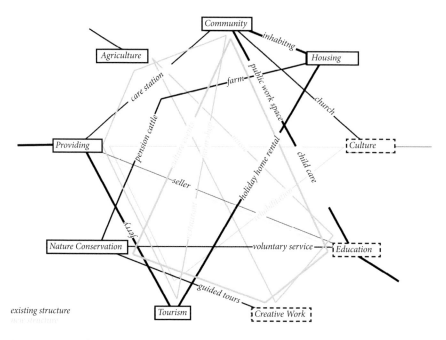

existing structure

new structure

Programming interrelations

Breathing in

Breathing out

As part of the natural processes in the Wadden Sea ecosystem, the Halligen have always been regularly flooded (*Land Unter*) and in a constant process of change. However, since climate change has caused sea levels to rise faster and extreme weather events to occur more frequently, the damage has become greater and life on the Halligen and their *warften* (artificial hills for farmsteads) more dangerous. Not only are people's homes at risk, but also animal habitats and agriculture. Ecologically, as well as culturally, they are an important habitat that needs new approaches in order to be preserved.

Currently, there are ten Halligen, stretching between the islands of Pellworm and Sylt. Most of them are connected to the mainland by regular ferry services, others by road dams. Some, such as Süderoog, can only be reached by boat at high tide and on foot over the mud-flats at low tide. Since the natural habitat of the Halligen are shaped by the tides, they have a high ecological diversity, with various plants and nutritious soil, making them an important habitat for migratory birds. The regular flooding is crucial for the growth of the Hallig through sedimentation, naturally adapting to rising sea levels. The problem, however, is that sedimentation does not take place fast enough in relation to the rise in sea levels. Among the elements to ensure the further existence of the Halligen are breakwaters and low dikes preventing the sediments of the Hallig from being washed away. In the past, this protection was abandoned, and people extracted salt peat, which brought the region its former prosperity, but also made the area vulnerable and led to several flood disasters. For a sustainable, resilient transformation, the transfer of this traditional and often tacit knowledge into future innovation is necessary. Looking at a map of the former settlements, the dikes and the former coastline is visible. For centuries, people have built their houses by the coast on elevations to protect them from floods. The *warften* made of peat soil, are an old form of settlement that continues to disappear. The architectural typology of the *warft* is a dense ensemble that includes rainwater reservoirs. The houses are arranged at the edge and provide an open space in the centre, which is protected from the wind and can either be used in the event of a storm surge to bring the livestock to safety or serve as a gathering area. When the storm surge comes, the *warft* is the only place where life is possible, temporarily creating high-density living.

As a scenario, structural measures can make the *warften* physically and socially resilient to climate change. They are "no-regret measures" that can be extended or adapted to changing conditions. One idea is the extension of *warften*, increasing the density of the existing building structures. Built in a way that they can continue to withstand the rise in sea level, they grow with it through sedimentation, which gives more space for additional programmes. Another idea is to strengthen the existing *warften*, as well as the programmes and community on the Hallig to create new offers that increase the liveability on the islands. For example, in the case of Hallig Hooge, a comparatively well-developed infrastructure (school, supermarket, fire station, community health station) can be connected with other islands to densify the network of programme components. Currently separated cycles of agriculture, fishery, local production, knowledge can be merged into a circular system.

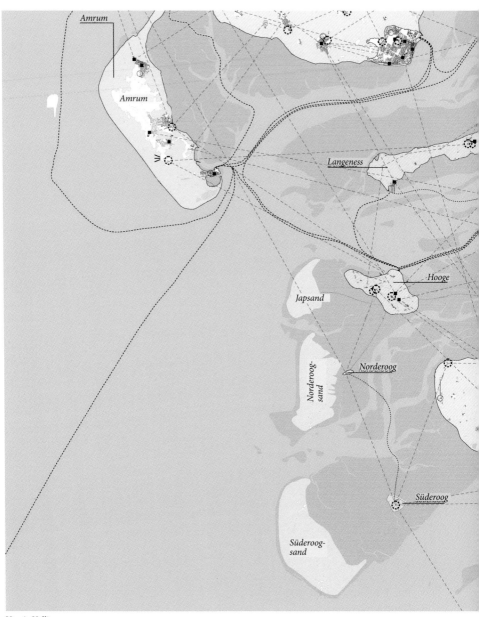

Amrum

Amrum

Langeness

Hooge

Japsand

Norderoog-
sand

Norderoog

Süderoog

Süderoog-
sand

Utopia Halligen

and

Ockholm

Gröde

Hamburger Hallig

Nordstrandischmoor

Pellworm

Südfall

five kilometres

SEASIDE

Living on the Coast

Alissa Diesch

Coasts are home to half of the global population. Iconic cities, important industries, and logistical hubs are to be found there, and coasts are also the most popular tourist destination. The interface of land and sea has always been the breeding ground for human evolution and innovation. Coastlines are marked by manifold forms of connecting, segregating, and hybridising land and sea, inland and coast, and different countries. Cliffs, dykes, and fortifications represent strong delimitations, while ports, beaches, fishing, lagoons, deltas, and energy production reflect exchanges that exist between the elements.

The sea and the land provide a confluence of products and backgrounds that empower the rise of hybrid cultures, emerging trends, and novel combinations, as can be seen in gastronomy, for example. This evolutionary character can be perceived in manifold urban typologies such as harbour towns, fishing villages, villas, vacation resorts, and many more. Harbours are gateways that connect to local and large-scale environments. The culture and architecture of port cities are therefore marked by the exchange their harbours embody as nodes in a global network (Hein 2011). Even small towns, locally perceived as provincial, have unexpectedly global, strongly influential relations through their port facilities (Diesch, Hansen 2021). Port cities as interfaces of exchange and mobility enable new readings of networks and coherencies.

Research and cultural projects explore how these relations can be read, deepened, and re-interpreted, for instance at the Baltic Sea (Djurdjevic, Paturet 2015) or the Mediterranean (OMA 2018; Ricci, Mantelli 2020). Multi-scalar relations support a polyvalent habitat in seaside areas that can be used for the creative reinvention of public space and new urban design paradigms (e. g., Gausa, Banchini, Falcón 2009). Clearly, tourism is a decisive factor in (trans-)forming places on many coasts and its different concepts strongly influence urban structures (Lanz, Wolfrum 2008). Trends in tourism like relational tourism are diversifying the field, and seasonal and multi-local living models are emerging in coastal areas. These new societal dynamics and subsequent spatial requirements can be used as drivers for urban change and the transformation of existing structures. The cultural background of multi-scalar and diverse relations, as well as the attractive natural spaces, achieve new possibilities through digital remote-working modes and temporary project collaborations. The different forms of urban and territorial configurations on the coast have been the focus of the Master Territorial Design Studio study *Seaside*. Settlement patterns here can be seen as stage for ongoing processes of metropolitan and touristic extension—therefore a main field for sustainable urban transformation and resilience. For this, coast stripes of 50 km x 20 km have been selected for a transversal analysis and scenarios. All stripes address territories beyond metropolitan cores. Overarching challenges such as rising sea levels and climatic, ecological, social, cultural, and economic changes were tackled at a territorial, urban, and architectural scale. Systematic and comparative mapping revealed the relation of existing places, structures, and socio-economic change. Since the studio was organised as a platform for exchange, where the students presented and discussed their findings, common topics could be identified and new knowledge was generated in a co-creative way. Activating and enhancing this background and the respective architecture as a resource, the students were keen to explore how vibrant and dynamic places and communities in peripheral, remote, and marginalised areas could evolve, exploring and inventing new spaces at the sea/land interface.

Seven case studies are developed as projective explorations that merge analytical and synthetic aspects in a stream of creative inventiveness. This methodology builds on concepts and tools of "strategic portraits" (Schröder, Sommariva 2017). The seven case studies form an overall taxonomy of deeply transformed coastal territories, organised and driven by projection towards resilience (Schröder, Diesch 2022).

Bibliography:

Diesch A., Hansen J. (2021) "From Harbour to Harbour: Postcolonial Relations and Agencies". In: *CPCL European Journal of Creative Practices in Cities and Landscapes*, 4 (1), pp. 40–59.

Djurdjevic M., Paturet T. (2015) *Atlas of Overexploited Territories. Baltic Sea*. Lausanne, École Polytechnique Federale de Lausanne.

Gausa M., Banchini S., Falcón L. (2009) *International Symposium Tourism XXL*. Barcelona, Edition Intelligent Coast.

Hein C., ed. (2011) *Port Cities. Dynamic Landscapes and Global Networks*. London, Routledge.

Lanz M., Wolfrum S. (2008) "A Toda Costa". In: Wolfrum S., Nerdinger W., Schaubeck S., eds. (2008) *Multiple City*. Berlin, JOVIS.

OMA (2018) *Palermo Atlas. Manifesta 12*. Milano, Humboldt Books.

Ricci M., Mantelli M. (2020) "Le Vie del Mediterraneo (MedWays)". In: *EcoWebTown Journal of Sustainable Design* 22/2020, pp. 80–84.

Schröder J., Sommariva E., eds. (2017) *Coast Portraits. Research and Strategies in Territorial Architecture*. Hannover, Regionales Bauen und Siedlungsplanung, Leibniz Universität Hannover.

Schröder J., Diesch A., eds. (2021) *Mountains. Habitat Explorations*. Hannover, Regionales Bauen und Siedlungsplanung, Leibniz Universität Hannover.

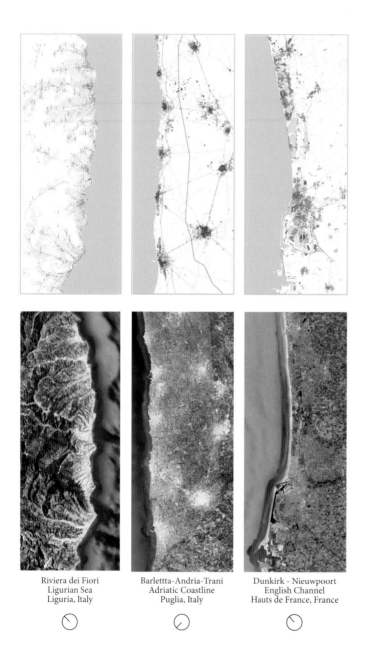

Riviera dei Fiori
Ligurian Sea
Liguria, Italy

Barlettta-Andria-Trani
Adriatic Coastline
Puglia, Italy

Dunkirk - Nieuwpoort
English Channel
Hauts de France, France

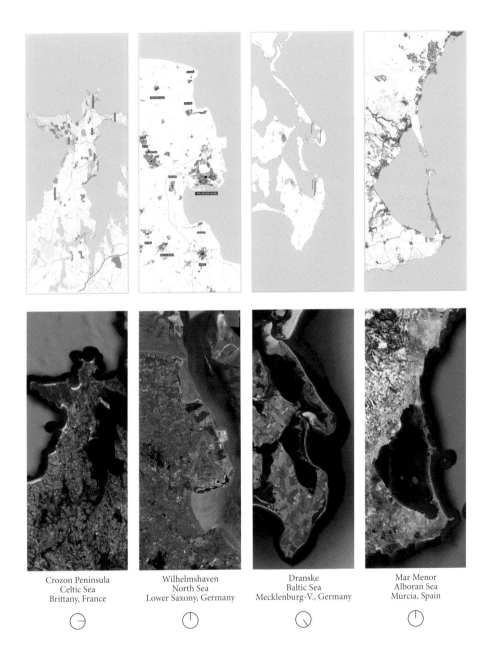

Crozon Peninsula
Celtic Sea
Brittany, France

Wilhelmshaven
North Sea
Lower Saxony, Germany

Dranske
Baltic Sea
Mecklenburg-V., Germany

Mar Menor
Alboran Sea
Murcia, Spain

Riviera dei Fiori

Leonardo Stadler and Max Passgang

Concept map

New places of mobility

Texts by Leonardo Stadler, Max Passgang, and Riccarda Cappeller

The smaller towns and villages in the mountains rising directly from the coast of the Riviera dei Fiori have been shrinking or abandoned for quite some time. Together with the high seasonal fluctuation directly on the coast, which is overcrowded in the summer, this causes frictions, contrasts, imbalances, and unsustainable neglect of resources and space. The project addresses these challenges by creating new circular dynamics through the recycling of existing buildings and networks, together with new connectivity along the coast and with the inland towns and villages. It aims to strengthen local communities that have already started new local production cycles, collective action, and cultural programmes.

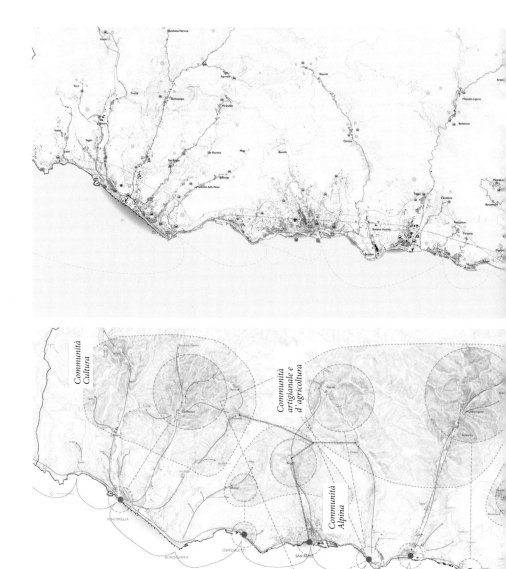

Analysis and vision "dai palmizi ai pini" (from the palms to the pines)

two kilometres

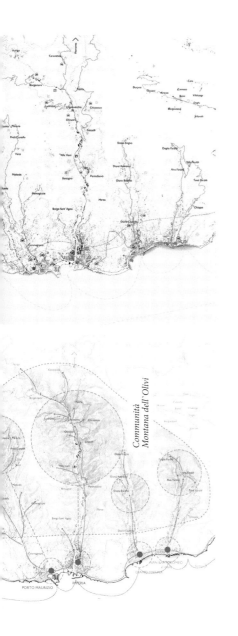

Communità Montana dell'Olivi

The Riviera dei Fiori is a coastal area between the cities of Cervo and Ventimiglia, connected with the ancient Roman coastal road Via Aurelia. The inland is characterised by the mountain range of the Ligurian Alps that give shelter against the winds and create the best growing conditions for early vegetables, wine grapes, and especially flowers and olives, which are important for the economy of the riviera. Tourism profits from the mild climate, and tourist activities are increasing. Nevertheless, the region is facing problems, such as the migration of the young population, structural change, and mobility and infrastructural provision in the inland areas. A major transformation in the last years was the closing of the old coastal railway, which left several stations in the centres of the cities abandoned. This railway line was planned to become a bicycle highway, but is still unfinished. Further inland, the new high-speed line Genova-Marseille will not connect the coastal cities.

The focus of this project is new linkages between the coast cities and the inland tows and villages, understanding the neglected areas as a major resource for overall sustainable perspectives of the area. The idea of the "moving city", developed by Archigram, serves as a model to use mobile and temporary events to transform places and to create a new network. Here, instead of taking the metropolis to peripheral places, as Archigram proposed, the mountains and its towns are brought into the city. Festivals are linked to rural economy, culture, and traditions such as seasonal harvests or local and nature-based products.

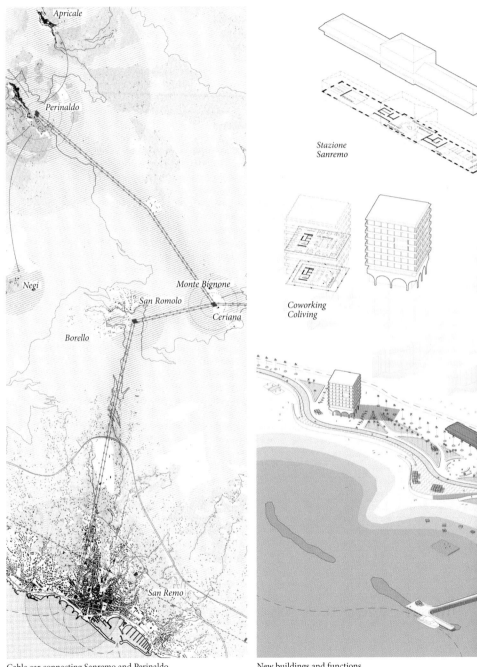

Apricale

Perinaldo

Negi

Monte Bignone

San Romolo

Ceriana

Borello

San Remo

Stazione
Sanremo

Coworking
Coliving

Cable car connecting Sanremo and Perinaldo

New buildings and functions

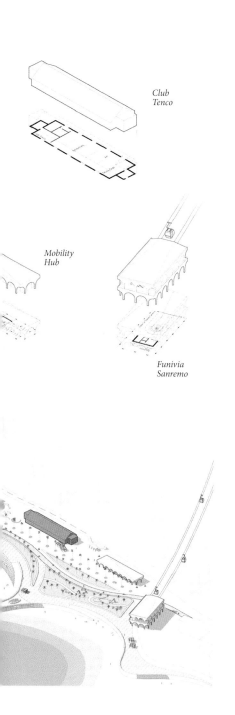

Club
Tenco

Mobility
Hub

Funivia
Sanremo

The festival starts in Ventimiglia at the beginning of every year and ends in San Bartolomeo al Mare, using the old railway infrastructure to move along the coast. Along this line, the project foresees a new cultural axis with car-free mobility, re-using the railway stations as new sustainable mobility hubs and reconnecting them. Each station is thought of as a place for social and cultural programmes, and is linked to one of the towns and villages inland. Here, thematic clusters and the bioregions of the valleys, identified in the mapping analysis, are to become platforms for new communities of circular economy.

Exemplarily, the scenario for the three valleys surrounding the city of Sanremo in the form of a horseshoe, not only sets these valleys into a new focus but creates new impulses for the city itself, now monostructurally oriented to its casino and yacht marina. Although the valleys are geographically near it, there is no linkage to the city. A shutdown cable car line is proposed to be reactivated and extended in order to connect to Sanremo from the town of Perinaldo in the mountains. Based on defining the strengths of Perinaldo, programmes foresee new sustainable touristic and educational activities and public spaces integrated into the historic centre. In Sanremo, besides the cable-car station on the coast, the railway station can be transformed into a creative hub with co-living and co-working possibilities to encourage young people to remain in the area. Along the waterfront that links both of these buildings to the larger framework of the cultural axis, a promenade facilitates the access to the sea and allows multiple sports and cultural activities in front of the former station, as an accessible and open urban space.

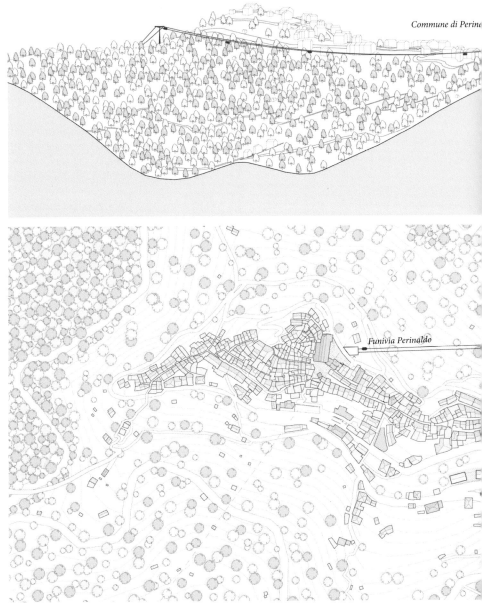

Commune di Perin

Funivia Perinaldo

Implementing new programmes in Perinaldo

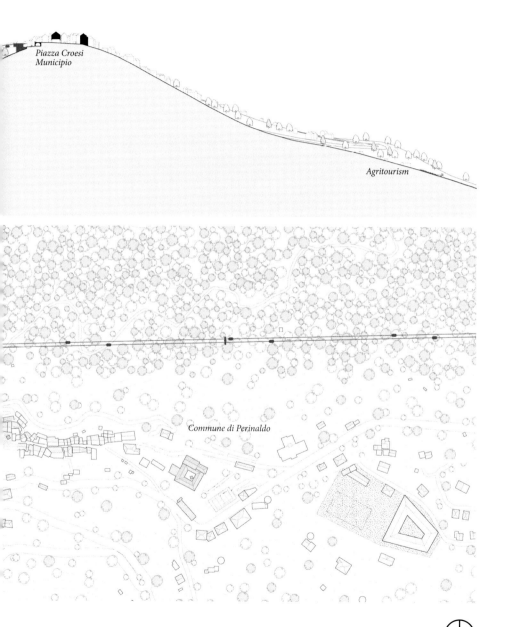

Piazza Croesi
Municipio

Agritourism

Commune di Perinaldo

one hundred metres

Welcome to Rügen

Maya Eberle and Malin Osterheider

Vision of the recycled prefabricated buildings

Texts by Maya Eberle, Malin Osterheider, and Jörg Schröder

Welcome to Rügen, one of the most popular touristic spots in Germany, with twice as many guests per inhabitant as Mallorca. And—not only due to COVID-19 but also due to an increasing demand for affordable and sustainable holidays—tourism numbers at the Baltic Sea coast in Germany are rising. The question is whether a claim of sustainability and natural and cultural values can correspond to reality, considering the extension of large-scale touristic facilities and infrastructure, the impact on local communities, and the increasing number of off-season ghost towns. To address these questions we zoom to the north of Rügen.

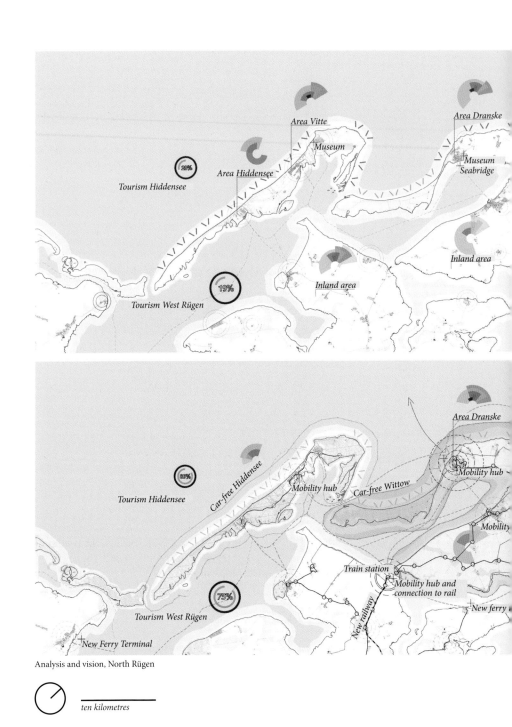

Analysis and vision, North Rügen

ten kilometres

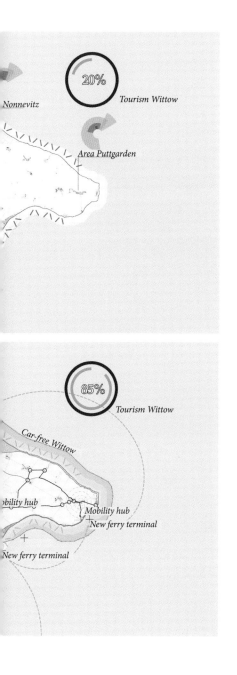

20%

Tourism Wittow

Nonnevitz

Area Puttgarden

85%

Tourism Wittow

Car-free Wittow

bility hub

Mobility hub

New ferry terminal

New ferry terminal

In the nineteenth century, fishing, agriculture, livestock breeding, trade, and pilotage were sources of income for the people of Rügen. In 1816, the first seaside resort was built, the era of tourism on the island started and became a new source of income. By the 1920s, Rügen was one of the most popular touristic destinations in Germany. Touristic architecture and infrastructure changed the towns. In order to cope with the rising number of tourists after the Second World War, prefabricated mass housing blocks were built on the island. Following the reunification of Germany in 1990, a new building boom began, which is ongoing and even increasing today. The mass tourism of the communist period era was followed by a new wave of tourism, with increasing tensions between nature conservationists, local activists, construction speculators, and tourism companies.

The island of Rügen is currently struggling with a decline in population and reduced social infrastructure, an increase in catchment areas for services, and rising costs, making permanent residence less attractive. In contrast, tourist visits to Rügen are steadily increasing: an increase of 93% from 1995 to 2017. The public transport system has been expanded in recent years and cycling and hiking trails have been created. Nevertheless, the preferred means of transport is still the car. The current bed-occupancy rate in the north of Rügen is only about 20% over the year due to large differences between high and low season.

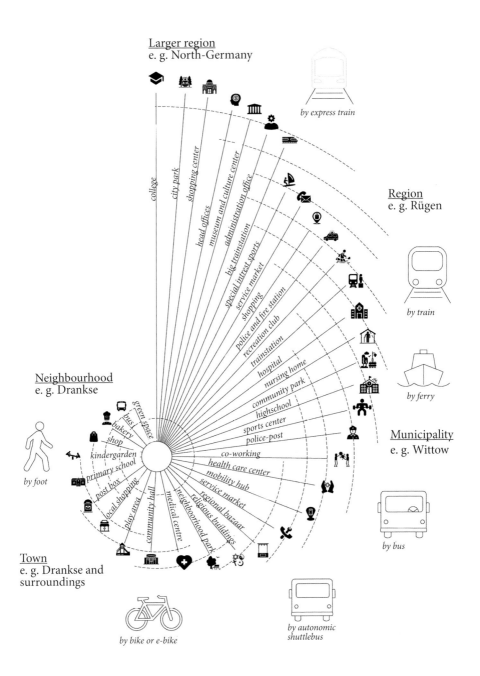

Larger region
e. g. North-Germany

by express train

Region
e. g. Rügen

by train

Neighbourhood
e. g. Drankse

by foot

by ferry

Municipality
e. g. Wittow

by bus

Town
e. g. Drankse and
surroundings

by bike or e-bike

by autonomic
shuttlebus

college
city park
shopping center
head offices
museum and culture center
administration office
big trainstation
special intrest sports
service market
shopping
police and fire station
recreation club
trainstation
hospital
nursing home
community park
highschool
sports center
police-post
co-working
health care center
mobility hub
service market
regional bazaar
religious buildings
neighboorhood park
medical centre
community hall
play area
local shopping
post box
primary school
kindergarden
shop
bakery
bus
green space

Mobility concept for North Rügen

Creative Lab

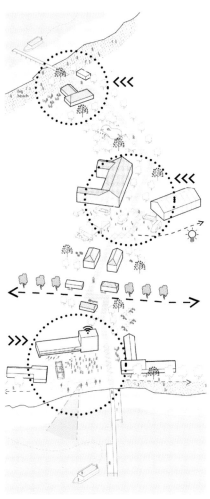

The starting point for this project is the plan to build a mega resort on the Bug peninsula in the north of Rügen. Analysing its eventual character as a gated community, its massive impact on nature, and its low benefit for the overall sustainable future of the island, the focus of the study is on exploring an alternative: to activate and densify the nearby town Dranske within a holistic development strategy for the tourism region of North Rügen.

Dranske's location between the Bodden lagoon and the open sea has major potential for new connectivity by boat and bicycle, as part of a car-free model region. Nature as a major attraction needs to be preserved and thus settlement limited to its borders. To achieve this, a deep analysis of the existing structures of Dranske leads to the identification of potential for activation and densification. Organised in phases of intervention, the project starts from a new arrival point for public boat transport as a mobility hub and a creative quarter in the recycled prefabricated housing blocks. It offers opportunities for digital work, fabrication with natural resources, and for new living-working models over the course of the year.

The axis between the pier at the Bodden and a new pier on the open sea is developed as an attractive urban space for pedestrians and cyclists. Along the axis, the town centre is activated by new cultural and productive uses. Thus, the project proposes new living and working forms, a new vision of time over the year, and to strengthen the creative potential of Rügen, in particular by recycling the existing prefabricated buildings and setting it in new relation to urban activities, to nature, and to the Baltic Sea.

Functional axis

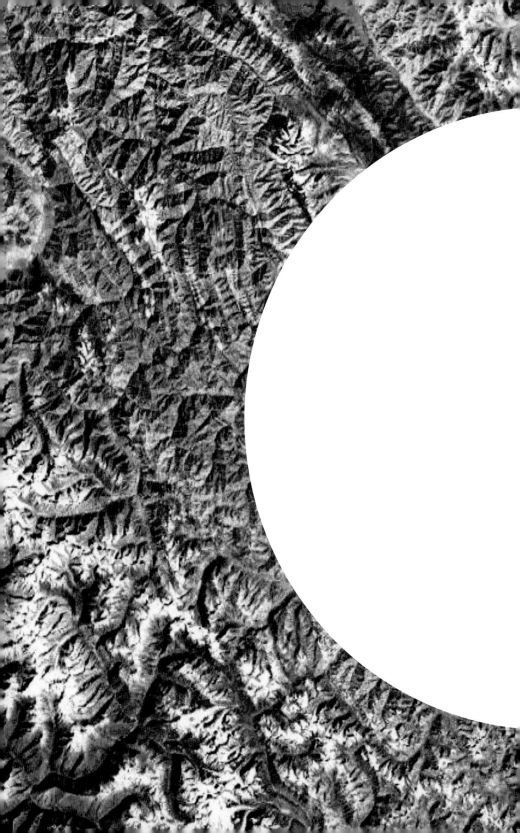

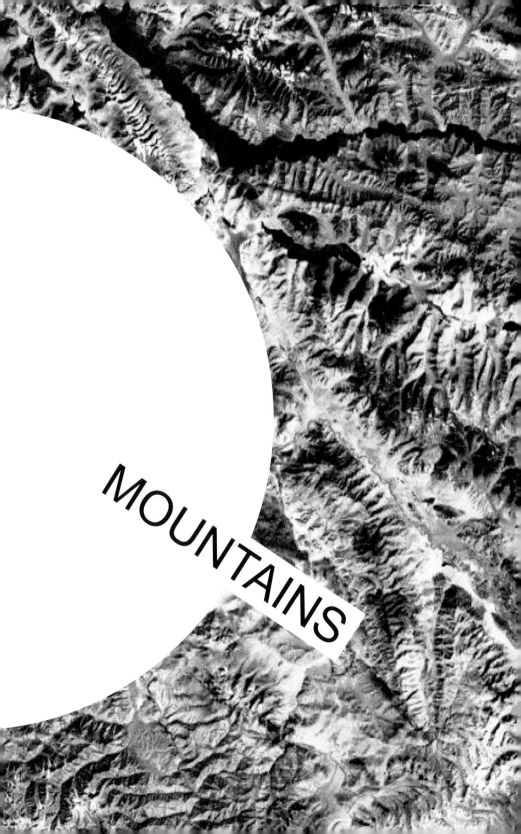

MOUNTAINS

Mountain Flows

Alissa Diesch and Jörg Schröder

In many global contexts, mountains are closely interconnected with and related to urban phenomena and urban agglomerations, with different flows, rhythms, linkages, and spatial expressions. Mountains are part of a diverse range of metropolitan agglomerations and urban networks in touristic areas or along infrastructural axes, as well as long-standing patterns of towns and villages. Nevertheless, topography, and climate too, constitute important aspects when approaching mountains, in particular with buildings and settlements that are influenced by these factors.

Different scales guide our understanding of mountains, ranging from urban mountains such as Collserola or Etna, to valleys as habitats, to larger territorial contexts such as el Alto, the Bavarian Alps, Grisons, or even the Alps as a whole. In this larger picture, cities and urban influence have been co-creators of a space shaped by humans for millennia, right up to the Anthropocene, whose impact is causing the shrinking of glaciers and other deep impact in mountain areas. The Alps, Andes, and even the Himalayas have been transitory areas and are in constant exchange with close by and far away metropolises. Places and people are in a dynamic interrelation that is not fixed or constant. One example of adaptation and movements in mountains is transhumance, the seasonal movement of humans and livestock between different places. This concept can be read as a rural form of a multi-local lifestyle in parallel with urban multi-localities due to commerce, education, religion, the military, administration, and tourism, which suggest that one should analyse and understand settlements in the mountains with a combined approach of detecting flows and territorial dimensions beyond single places.

The reading of the Alps, in particular, as places of longing, with a stunning panorama of peaks and valleys, began with industrialisation. An imaginary was cultivated where mountains are seen as extreme and fascinating territories in contrast to cities, linked to activities such as sports, anthropology, or architecture. From the perspective of "vernacular intelligence" (Schröder 2017), the particular topographical and climatic conditions of summits, valleys, hills, and mountain ranges globally have been the breeding ground for highly adapted lifestyles, cultures, settlement, and building patterns. Relations between humans and nature, but also relations between rural and urban traits, or between local and global are referred to as the "good life" (Bätzing 2009; Biedowicz, Friedrich, Ríos Aramayo 2016) and earmarked as models of sustainable living—as opposed to the touristic, infrastructural, military, or mining characteristics of mountains.

Today, metropolisation is provoking an exodus of the local population as well as movements of re-settlement, and not only in remote areas but also near to agglomerations. These pheonomena are often interrelated with tourism and updated models of contemporary transhumance based on digital remote working and temporary project collaborations. Emerging life and work models are already setting novel trends on the peripheries, revaluing and making use of existing structures by enhancing them with spatial, cultural, technical, and social innovation (Schröder et al. 2018). Switching the perspective, understanding the relations of peripheral areas of mountains and adjacent cities from a different angle, can reveal overlooked dynamics and trigger new concepts for living and work (Diesch 2020).

The Master Studio *Mountains* addressed prospects for different mountain contexts. The project began with detecting and systematically mapping characteristics and potentials of spaces to adapt, modify, and enhance them with new concepts, taking into account a variety of trends and dynamics. Communities living in the mountains were examined for adaptive concepts for organising life, work and culture, integrating and generating innovation (Schröder, Diesch 2021). These spatial, social, cultural, and economic structures are as characteristic and important for the places as the topographical context. Rediscovered and updated models of intertwining living and work spaces are elaborated, considering existing and new inhabitants. Furthermore, the projects carved out the creative capacity of these territories by inventing original and promising concepts based on their specific spatial and social characteristics.

Bibliography:

Bätzing W. (2009) *Orte guten Lebens: Die Alpen jenseits von Übernutzung und Idyll.* Zürich, Rotpunktverlag.

Biedowicz M., Friedrich M., Ríos Aramayo D. (2016) *Vivir Bien / Buen Vivir / Das gute Leben. Artes Contemporáneas de Latinoamérica / Zeitgenössische Kunst aus Lateinamerika.* La Paz, Museo Nacional de Arte and Goethe Institut.

Diesch A. (2020) "Trueque Based Urbanism". In: Schröder J., Sommariva E., Sposito S., eds. (2020) *Creative Food Cycles. Book 1.* Hannover, Leibniz Universität Hannover. pp. 106–115.

Schröder J. (2017) "The Construction of Alpine Building Culture". In: *ALPS design magazine* 2017(1), pp. 14–21

Schröder J., Carta M., Ferretti M., Lino B., eds. (2018) *Dynamics of Periphery. Atlas of Emerging Creative and Resilient Habitats.* Berlin, JOVIS.

Schröder J., Diesch A., eds. (2021) *Mountains. New Habitat Explorations.* Hannover, Regionales Bauen und Siedlungslanung, Leibniz Universität Hannover.

Iseo Lake
Italy

Thuringa
Germany

Harz
Germany

Sarn Valley
Italy

Soča Valley
Slovenia

Crimea
Ukraine

Leukerbad
Switzerland

Bergell and Engadin
Switzerland

Sagarmatha
Nepal

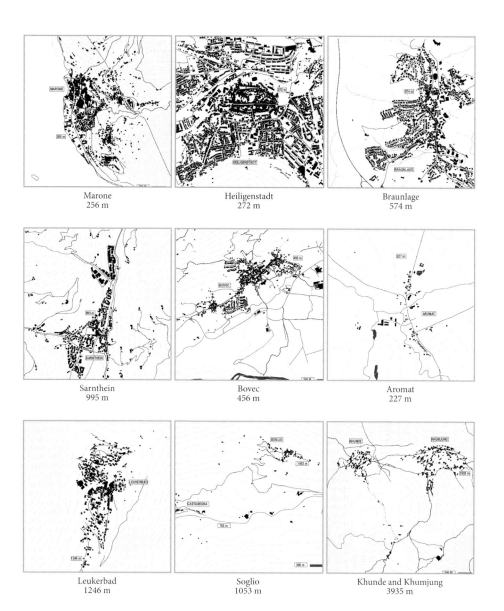

Marone
256 m

Heiligenstadt
272 m

Braunlage
574 m

Sarnthein
995 m

Bovec
456 m

Aromat
227 m

Leukerbad
1246 m

Soglio
1053 m

Khunde and Khumjung
3935 m

Collserola Ring

Michel Grändorf

Serra de Collserola, Spain

Ciutat Meridiana, 153 m

Texts by Michel Grändorf, Alissa Diesch, and Jörg Schröder

If we understand the Serra de Collserola mountains as a player in the metropolitan game around Barcelona, new perspectives for territorial innovation can be gained. The vision of a polycentric urban ring around the mountains, based on a circular tramway, can activate and diversify existing centralities. It could become a gateway to the mountains and thus support their vitality. We need to link regional analysis, territorial visioning, and mobility planning to urban planning and architecture, bound together in a design approach that aims for sustainability and is driven by the recycling of town centres around Serra de Collserola.

Public space in the town centre of El Papiol

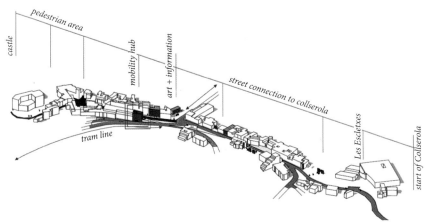

New connectivity in the town centre of El Papiol

Vision for the mobility station in El Papiol

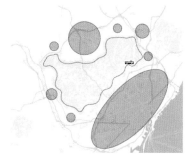

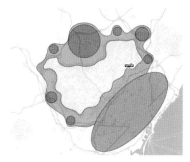

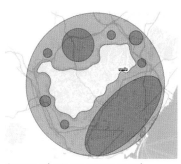

Ongoing urbanisation process around
Collserola, turned into a ring concept

The Serra de Collserola mountains are inland in the north-west of Barcelona, and during the last decades have been surrounded by metropolitan expansion up to the urbanised inland valley of Vallès, parallel to the coast. In this expansion, the historic centres of the small towns around Collserola have lost their prior function and are becoming decoded spaces, open to the inscription of new vitality and vocation. Three approaches can guide an exploration of this potential: first, the idea of polycentric poles with new social, cultural, and—in terms of circular economy—productive and commercial function, supported by digital possibilities and the desire for urbanity that overcomes the diffuse living model of the past. Second, giving a new centrality to the territory, bound to lighter forms of mass transport such as tramways, induced by the necessary shift to sustainable mobility. And third, the idea of creating gateways for the Collserola mountains that can support the experience of their ecological role as a green lung, for heat mitigation, biodiversity through a cultural and social dimension: discovering the many cultural places in the mountains, the topic of agriculture, and of natural resources for a circular economy. These three lines of investigation serve to focus the project's analysis and identify the diverse and sometimes contradictory frameworks, actor constellations, and ways of doing of the until now separate fields of reference. The hypothesis of the project is to bring the three fields radically together, starting from a vision of the town centres around Collserola as places for a new habitat, sustainable lifestyles, and new activities. They become nodes for new ecological, economic, social, but also cultural flows in the metropolitan region.

Urban carpet

In the towns around the Serra de Collserola, the implementation of new multi-modal mobility points with the tramway as backbone can be interrelated with the activation of the town centres, not only in a multifunctional sense and as places of proximity, but also with new central functions as multiple exchange and access nodes for the urbanised metropolitan area. Not least, the tramway is a gateway to reach Collserola by public transport, offering information, education, events. The project examines two case studies around Collserola to exemplify the potentials of the project: El Papiol in the west and Ciutat Meridiana in the east. While the first is a historically grown town, the latter is a high-rise suburb of residential and industrial use built in the second half of the twentieth century and is selected to show the transferability of the concept beyond traditional centralities.

El Papiol, with its historic centre, recent housing neighbourhoods and industrial zones, can serve as example of a small town overrun by metropolitan expansion, deeply linked by commuting and other streams to Barcelona. In particular the town centre lacks a role in the larger metropolitan game, barely relating to the nearby Collserola mountains. The mobility point of the ring tramline in the town centre is designed as a hub and connector to the urban and natural attractions. It offers views towards the castle and the Collserola. The building hosts gastronomic and cultural offers and links the station with the town on different topographic levels. The tramline also supports the activation and recycling of buildings in the town centre along the axis to the castle, converted into pedestrian and bicycle areas, highlighted by a continuous pavement—an urban carpet.

MEDWAYS

Medways: Circular Territories

Jörg Schröder

The research project *Medways: Circular Territories* (Schröder et al. 2022) is an invitation to a journey exploring the Mediterranean as a cultural space that is constantly changing and connecting. The project aims to find new creative and designerly methods to extend circular economies towards territorial innovation. *Medways: Circular Territories* is a part of the international research project *Medways* at the Italian Academy of Sciences dei Lincei, directed by Mosè Ricci (2022). *Medways* understands the Mediterranean as a space of flows and at the same time as a fragile habitat that faces common challenges: how to turn climate change and migration into opportunities for resilience and innovation, linked with the question of how to foster creativity and to use cultural heritage, and how to open up through this combination new cultural, social, ecological, and economic perspectives.

The starting point for the project is to observe bottom-up innovations and how they are already being connected. Enterprises such as Orange Fiber (Santonocito, Arena 2019) realise the green transition by opening-up cross-cutting inventions between research, design, and production. Their patented sensorial fabric is created by transforming citrus juice by-products into a silk-like cellulose yarn. With 700,000 tons of citrus by-products dealt with as waste in Italy every year, this example connects to an increasing innovation network, but also to a successful branding based on the knowledge and culture of the Mediterranean in order to enact a circular economy. This framework offers to decouple prosperity from the consumption of finite resources: bioeconomy can become a driver for sustainable production systems and creator of local value loops. *Circular Territories* is a culture- and creativity-based approach for innovation and resilience aiming to create and enhance the dynamic interaction of ideas, people, and space—oriented to circular principles.

Circular Design (Schröder 2020) grasps and shapes material and immaterial circular dynamics. With particular attention to bio-economy, digitalisation, and cultural industries, this project asks how innovative urbanism and architecture can contribute to the enhancement of a circular economy in cities and territories, and how, on the other hand, a circular economy and circular principles can become a driver for the urban and territorial transformation to sustainability. The case studies shown here, originating in a seminar, are based on a research and design approach that combines creativity and methodological precision in innovative tools. In the first part, mapping and diagramming capture spatial potentials at the scales of territories/places/buildings, connecting settlement, infrastructures, and agriculture, and identifying existing circular approaches. Discovering the topic of the circular economy includes theoretical references as well as project examples.

In the second part, scenarios are drawn that articulate circular territories at different interconnected scales and with a focus on mechanisms and paradigms of circular practices—exploring their impact in space as well as reshaping territorial, economic, social, ecological, and cultural frameworks. The work is organised transversally in three case studies that connect Mediterranean metropolises with surrounding areas closely related to agricultural production: the area around Mount Etna and Catania (Sicily), the Terra di Bari and Bari (Apulia), and the basin of Guadalquivir and Seville (Andalusia).

It becomes clear that approaches need to be developed in a highly context-bound manner. Nevertheless, all three cases show that new networks of towns and enterprises can be inspired and driven by a circular spirit, which starts from using the by-products of food production processes but goes further to merge circular principles into territorial innovation. Movements of people and goods have been identified as crucial, linked with perception, access, and sustainable transport (train and bike ring; new links from the sea to the mountains; boats on the river) and combined with an activation of settlements, in particular town centres. New interaction between peripheries and metropolises is envisioned, with cross-cutting innovations induced by circular approaches. At the same time, the transversal perspective can lead to the identification of opportunities for transregional cooperation as well as for initiatives and policy innovation, brought to a wider level in the Mediterranean and beyond.

Bibliography:

Ricci M., Pasquali M., Mannocci S., eds. (2022) *Medways. Open Atlas*. Syracuse, LetteraVentidue Edizioni.

Schröder J. (2020) "Circular Design for the Regenerative City: A Spatial-digital Paradigm". In: Schröder J., Sommariva E., Sposito S., eds. (2020) *Creative Food Cycles. Book 1*. Hannover, Regionales Bauen und Siedlungsplanung, Leibniz Universität Hannover. DOI: http://doi.org/10.15488/10074, pp. 17–31.

Schröder J., Cappeller R., Diesch A., Scaffidi F. (2022) "Circular Territories. Culture-led approach for territorial innovation, resilence, and bio-economy". In: Ricci M., Pasquali M., Mannocci S., eds. (2022) *Medways. Open Atlas*. Syracuse, LetteraVentidue Edizioni, pp. 467–478.

Santonocito A., Arena E. (2019) "Orange Fiber". In: Markopoulou A., Farinea C., Ciccone F., Marengo M., eds. (2019) *Creative Food Cycles. Food Interaction Catalogue*. Barcelona, Institute of Advanced Architecture, pp. 224–227.

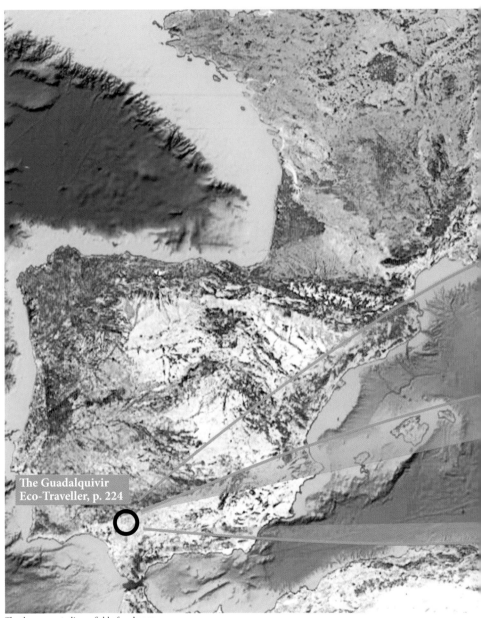

The Guadalquivir
Eco-Traveller, p. 224

The three case studies as field of exchange

The Terra di Bari
Experience, p. 214

Circular around
Etna, p. 204

two hundred kilometres

Circular around Etna

Gülce Erincik and Sarah Pens

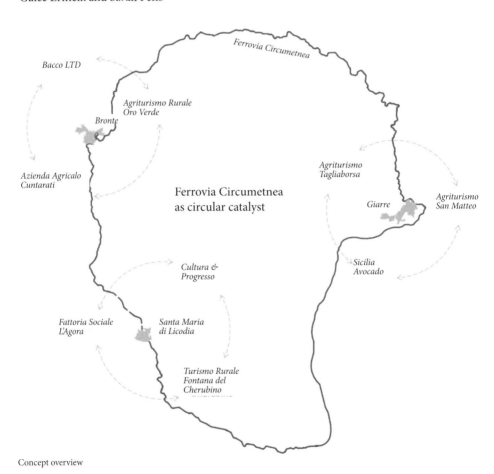

Concept overview

Texts by Gülce Erincik, Sarah Pens, and Jörg Schröder

This investigation aims to detect circular dynamics and their role in the interaction of the area around Mount Etna with the metropolis Catania. It discovers potential for the influence of a circular economy on a new habitat on the periphery as a vibrant and attractive living space. The food sector is and always has been very strong around Mount Etna due to fertile soil and the Mediterranean climate. A focus on bio-economy enables an exploration of cooperation between rural towns, farmsteads, and the city as well as cooperation between the research, agricultural, food, tourism, and mobility infrastructure sectors.

Regalbuto

Giumarra

Ramacca

Semi-open land
Mixed cultivation
High mountain natural
Mediterranean open land
Mountain forest
Intensive crops

ten kliometres

The investigation area of 50 by 50 km in-cludes Catania, the coastline to the Ionian Sea, the Simeto River Basin, and the area around Mount Etna—including towns and farmsteads, industrial areas, and in-frastructures in a metropolitan range. The fertile volcanic soils support intense agriculture, with vineyards and orchards spread along the lower slopes of the mountain and on the plain of Catania in the south. Mount Etna also plays a signi-ficant role in culture, especially in Greek mythology. As one of the tallest active volcanoes in Europe, it is among Sicily's main tourist attractions and a UNESCO World Heritage Site.

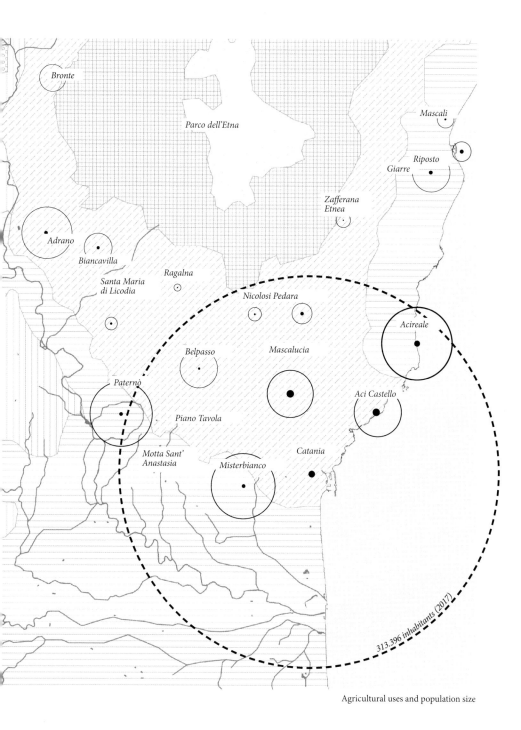

Agricultural uses and population size

Circular Around Catania aims to explore circular dynamics, based on bio-economy, between agriculture, the food sector, other sectors, and tourism. Initiatives, entrepreneurship, and actors in all these fields are present in the territory, but until now systemic and spatial interaction, as well as an expression of innovation in space, have developed in only a few cases. With a view to local and metropolitan development, the future of small towns and farmsteads can be inspired by circular dynamics—also connected to further topics such as education and, in particular, mobility infrastructure. In the investigated area, several studies and innovative companies are already developing approaches to a circular economy. For example, Bacco Ltd in Bronte works in pistachio production. During the transformation of pistachios into products, the shell becomes a by-product. It represents between 35% and 45% of the total weight of the fruit and therefore offers a potential to be used as an alternative source of energy (Raciti et al. 2020). In cooperation with the University of Catania, multiple possibilities are being developed (Chinnici 2019) for the use of citrus waste. The company Orange Fiber recycles *pastazzo* (the residue that remains at the end of the industrial production of citrus juice) to make yarn extracted from cellulose for use in the fashion sector. 60% of the original weight of the fruits is considered until now as a worthless by-product (Santonocito, Arena 2019).

The analysis leads to a design process that aims to develop exemplary circular systems that link and expand existing initiatives. The interventions focus on selected parts of the analysis, such as innovative companies in the bio-economy sector, agritourism, and community-oriented food systems (Mendez et al. 2021). Based on studies in several towns around Mount Etna, the existing railway line Ferrovia Circumetnea is found to have major potential not only for the sustainable mobility of people and goods between the rural areas and the metropolis, for workers, consumers, tourists, researchers, but also as an imaginative and branding element for new territorial cooperation. This existing connection is used as an element to develop circular systems further and to enhance existing local assets, potential, and values.

On this scale, the project starts with "closing the circle": since the railway ends in two stations very close to the main railway network, it does not yet have the ability to create a circular connection around Mount Etna. Therefore, these two gaps need to be closed. The line and vehicles require improvement, for higher frequency and capacity, so that even more towns around Etna can be connected. To strengthen the circular connectivity, a bicycle highway parallel to the train line is proposed.

In order to develop scenarios of circular systems, three cases studies have been chosen. They represent different aspects of the area, mainly in terms of agricultural production, but also with regard to the size and character of the settlement, the re-use of different types of farmsteads (*masserie*) and local initiatives. A four by four km square for the scenarios frames the towns and at least three existing places of innovation (two farmsteads and one company or association), to start a circular system and to promote the principles of a circular vocation. Flows in this system include materials, products, energy, but also ideas, knowledge, and financial aspects.

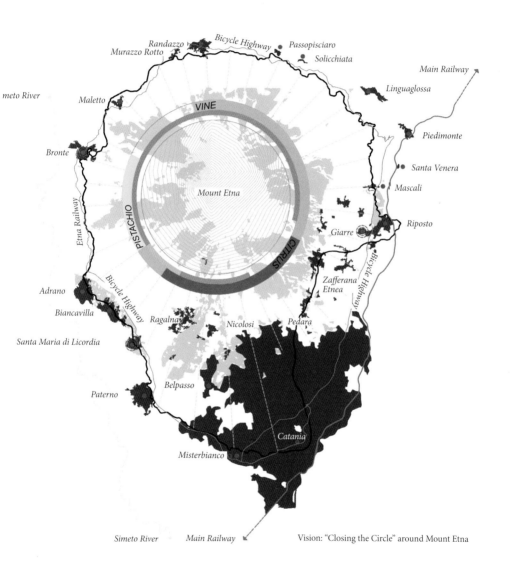

Vision: "Closing the Circle" around Mount Etna

Santa Maria di Licodia

Bronte

Giarre

New bicycle paths are introduced to link these points and to include cultural attractions. The station of the Ferrovia Circumetnea is seen as a mobility hub, connecting the bicycle and foot network with the railway and the bicycle highway, becoming a welcome and information centre and a gateway for products.

Bronte, the town of the pistachio, with 18,700 inhabitants is situated directly next to the Simeto River and the Etna National Park. The scenario starts with the company Bacco Ltd and the *masserie* Oro Verde and Cuntarati.

Giarre, with 27,400 inhabitants, is at the eastern slope of the Mount Etna. The company Sicily Avocado, the *masseria* Tagliaborsa, and the *masseria* San Matteo, an organic farm, are selected.

Santa Maria di Licodia, close to Catania, has 7,500 inhabitants and a former Benedictine Abbey, the association Cultura e Progresso, the *masseria* Fontana del Cherubino, and the *masseria* L'Agora, with a concept to enhance social and cultural functions of the farm.

Example Santa Maria di Licodia: Here, the new point of arrival, linked to the mobility hub, is foreseen as a social and cultural centre for the activities of the association Cultura e Progresso (Foundation with the South 2021) as part of the circular system. Its location in the town next to the sports ground offers opportunities to organise temporary markets and cultural events that promote local production and creativity. Awareness and knowledge of local heritage can be disseminated, and a higher level of visibility and communication can be achieved. The social farm L'Agora is foreseen as the educational and research centre in the proposed circular system. Since it is already based on a multifunctional concept, the project

aims to expand it with youth education. The farmhouse provides space for events, while the generous greenhouse and surrounding plantations are used for agricultural production. The complex is supplemented by sports facilities and smaller buildings. The vision is based on the idea of consistent flows that activate the area socially, economically, and culturally, based on existing capabilities and values in culture and ecology formed over many years. The goal is to develop an innovative approach that upgrades the existing situation, filling the blanks with a new type of user and new usages of spaces. The interventions support a novel cycle of more efficient and persistent elements. Foreseen new elements are a youth centre with hostel, further production and refinement facilities, and a space for events and workshops. Beyond the additions and the impulse to create new workflows between the existing elements, a new bicycle infrastructure is suggested on a small scale.

Bibliography:

Chinnici G., Zarbà C., Hamam M., Pecorino B. (2019) "A Model of Circular Economy of Citrus Industry". In: *19th International Multidisciplinary Scientific GeoConferences SGEM*, 2019(4)2.

Foundation with the South (2021) *The Culture & Progress Association 'Freedom is participation'*. Available online at: https://www.esperienzeconilsud.it/recapsimeto/2021/04/02/ cultura-progresso-liberta-partecipazione/ (01.06.2022).

Mendez G. R., Pappalardo G., Farrell B. (2021) "Practicing Fair and Sustainable Local Food Systems. Elements of Food Citizenship in the Simeto River Valley". In: *Agriculture* 2021, 11(1), 56.

Raciti R., Terranova E., Tuccio G., Zerbo A., Rey I (2020) "Bacco Ltd: Technological Innovations for Energy Recovery in the Bronte Pistachio Chain". In: *Procedia Environmental Science, Engineering, and Management* 7(2020) (2), pp. 223–231.

Santonocito A., Arena E. (2019) "Orange Fiber". In: Markopoulou A., Farinea C., Ciccone F., Marengo M., eds. (2019) *Creative Food Cycles. Food Interaction Catalogue*. Barcelona, Institute of Advanced Architecture, pp. 224–227. Available online at: https://iaac.net/wp-content/uploads/pdf/CFC_290719_HRinteractive_doublepageS_locked.pdf (01.06.2022).

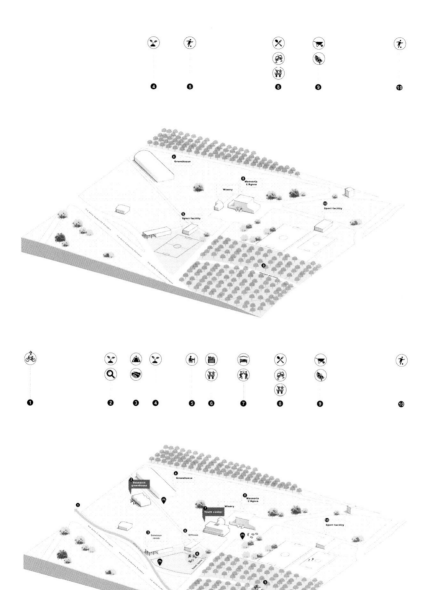

Masseria L'Agora: Existing structure and vision, programming, and interventions

The Terra di Bari Experience

Niccoló Huesmann, Jan Hüttmann, and Tamás Oravecz-Deák

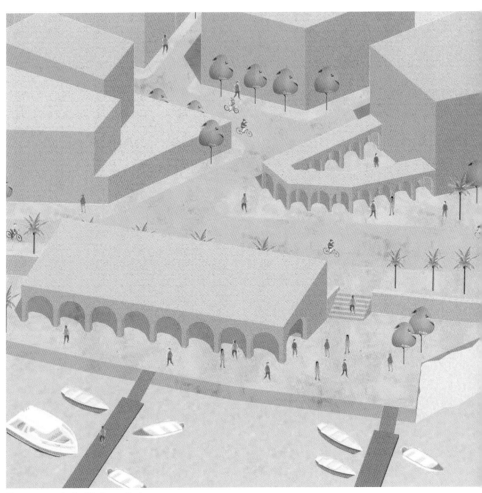

New structures in the Giovinazzo harbour area

Texts by Niccoló Huesmann, Jan Hüttmann, Tamás Oravecz-Deák, and Jörg Schröder

The Terra di Bari—known for its oil and wine production—extends from Bari to the north, including parts of the province Barletta-Andria-Trani. It is located along the Adriatic coast, with the Alta Murgia mountains in the south-west. The investigation into circular dynamics for new economic perspectives and a new habitat vision in the area starts from examining the characteristics of the area's long-running agricultural vocation and of its settlement structure. The focus is on bio-economy, in particular the use of food by-products for other sectors, the linkage to a more sustainable tourism, and new flows between the rural towns and the metropolitan city of Bari.

Residential
Commercial
Alta Murgia National Park
Olive fields
Adriatic Sea
Harbour Size
Topography (20m)

ten kliometres

From the point of view of food production, the area of 50 by 50 km can be
characterised by horizontal layers: first
the Adriatic coast with its fishery activities, then the oil and wine production,
and in the south-west the Alta Murgia
mountains. The settlement structure corresponds to this horizontal layout: a line
of towns along the coast, a second line
of towns in the agricultural inland, and
smaller dispersed places in the mountains.

Agriculture in the Terra di Bari

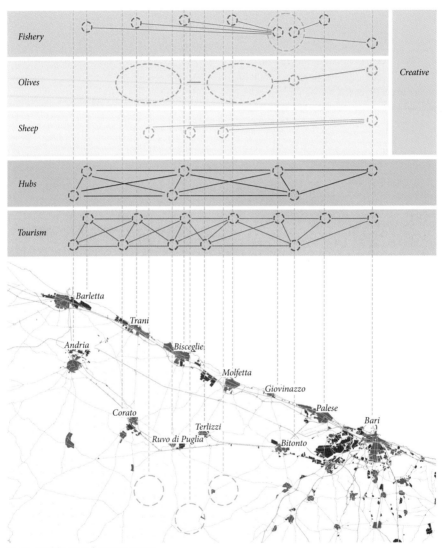

The layers of the *Terra di Bari Experience*

The Terra di Bari offers a rich cultural and historical heritage in its towns, architecture, and agricultural spaces. Thus it is not surprising that the region is a famous tourist destination, in particular the UNESCO World Heritage Site Castel del Monte in the south of Andria.

A horizontal layout of transport infrastructures can also be observed, with public transport by train and bus and the bicycle paths that are being installed in Apulia. Roads and train lines follow the horizontal set-up along the coast and further inland, with Bari as a gateway to national and international networks, by train, airplane, and ship. The well-maintained bicycle routes in the area connect the whole heel of Italy. The Alta Murgia National Park has two bike routes and various hiking paths. Vertical connections between the towns, from the sea to the inland and to the mountains, however, are overall neglected.

By turning the observation of layers into a concept, innovation in terms of creating a circular economy and territorial development can be targeted efficiently, and proposals for interventions can be defined accordingly. Furthermore, the concept of layers offers transversal strategies: in terms of cycles and flows of circular economy, new connectivity, and branding. While the blue strip (coast), the green strip (inland), and the yellow strip (mountains) show that circular economies benefit from the existing horizontal infrastructure, it is the hubs and the innovation in tourism that allow the concept to function more holistically. New hubs will be intermodal points of arrival and exchange, for people and for goods, in the concentrated settlement of the towns. From here, a new vertical connectivity can start.

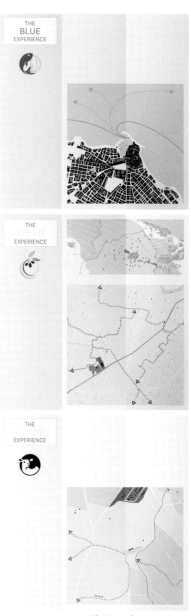

The Terra di Bari catalogue

A vision of sustainable tourism points on the one hand to the need to transform this important economic sector, and on the other hand sees tourism as a catalyst for change in the territory: for investment in infrastructures, for opening up fields of circular economy through new demand, and for advocating a sustainable branding beyond tourism marketing. Hence, the *Terra di Bari Experience* is meant as a process of local change and identification, as well as a pathway towards sustainable tourism.

The area will be activated by adding new vertical connections between the towns for people and for goods in of the form of light, adaptive, on-demand electronic vehicles and bicycle highways, accessible digitally for information and payment. Smart vertical connection from the coast to the mountains will attract more tourists concerned with sustainability, but will also connect local production chains, enterprises, and people, thus contributing the towns' attractiveness as living spaces, to stem the current move of young people to Bari or even further away, to the north of Italy and Europe. Many different circular economy approaches are already in motion in Apulia. Through spreading and enhancing projects of circular economy in the region, both the local economy and the environment will benefit. Corresponding to the concept of layers, scenarios for each of the strips start from connecting the existing towns and agricultural activities with circular ideas and with opportunities of sustainable tourism.

The **Blue Experience** will focus on the establishment of a circular fishing industry and economy in the coastal towns, which will ease the ongoing crisis of the fishery and declining communities. The

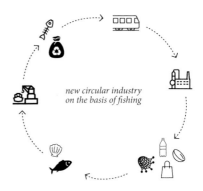

new circular industry on the basis of fishing

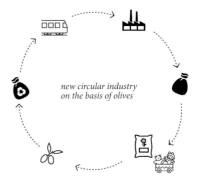

new circular industry on the basis of olives

re-etablishing the sheeppopulation for a future industry

Circular economy concepts: fish, olives, sheep

Giovinazzo harbour: satellite image and map

Bitonto olive fields: satellite image and map

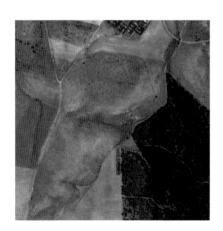

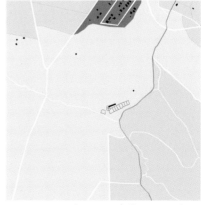

Alta Murgia: satellite image and map

A selection from the comic of the *Terra di Bari Experience*

recycling of fish waste and discarded nets will be one of the targets. Fish waste will be collected and transported to chemical plants, where a purification process will take place in order to produce biopolymers as a resource for several new end-products in different sectors.

The **Green Experience** will create sustainable cycles in the cultivation of olives, towards a new industry with factories and supply chains that focus on producing fertilisers and products in other sectors based on the waste from olive production.

Finally, the **Yellow Experience** will focus on saving the famous Alta Murgia sheep, which is endangered. The re-establishment of an ancient tradition in this area will create opportunities in sectors other than the food economy.

Overall, the scenarios show that the circular activation of current agricultural practices and of a rich cultural and ecological heritage can influence territorial development. Opportunities in production and tourism can be created, for example agritourism, sports activities, or guided tours accompanying the shepherds and their flocks along the tracks, taking part in harvesting olives, or fishing. As a part of the scenario-building approach, a comic tells the story of two visitors, a tourist from Germany and his local friend, who travel in the Terra di Bari of the future. It aims to transmit a narrative, atmospheres, and scenes created and achieved through the *Terra di Bari Experience*.

The Guadalquivir Eco-Traveller

Juan Esteban Hernandez Cardona, Vanessa Ehrich, and Melanie Oeltjen

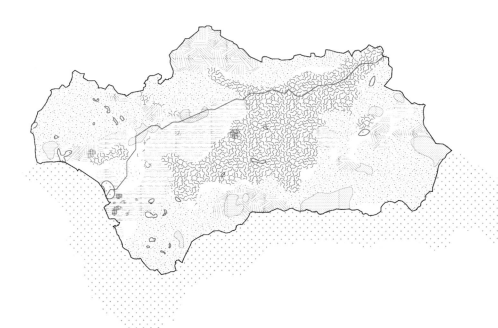

Agriculture in the Guadalquivir basin

Texts by Juan Esteban Hernandez Cardona, Vanessa Ehrich, Melanie Oetjen, and Jörg Schröder

The Guadalquivir basin around Seville has, since Phoenician, Greek, Roman, and Arab times, been an area of intense food production thanks to fertile soil, ample water, and good climate. Today, with climate change, a need to think and act differently arises. Innovation will be necessary and a circular economy can be taken as a paradigm to guide this transformation, in particular regarding linkages with Seville in terms of new production chains and financial and knowledge flows that strengthen the economy of the whole metropolitan region. The rural towns around Seville, in this process, can assume a new role in a circular network as places of metropolitan habitat.

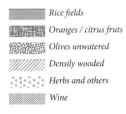

Rice fields
Oranges / citrus fruts
Olives unwatered
Densily wooded
Herbs and others
Wine

ten kliometres

According to the study *Desertnet II,* the Guadalquivir valley and its affluent rivers face a high risk of desertification, due to climate change and the intense use of the land and water. This challenge threatens the economic and social future of the region and in particular of the rural towns around Seville, in the middle of rice fields, citrus and olive plantations, but also vineyards and herb fields. The agricultural areas around Seville, some extended, some fragmented, embedded in complex metropolitan infrastructures and settlement patterns, offer the potential for strong interaction with the metropolis in an ecological and circular orientation not only of the food sector but of other sectors as well.

Agriculture and settlement around Seville

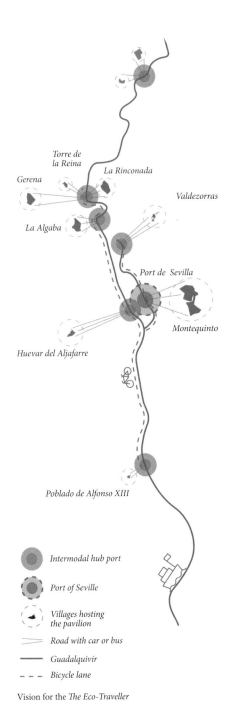

Torre de
la Reina

La Rinconada

Gerena

Valdezorras

La Algaba

Port de Sevilla

Montequinto

Huevar del Aljafarre

Poblado de Alfonso XIII

● Intermodal hub port

◉ Port of Seville

⌁ Villages hosting
the pavilion

⟩⟩ Road with car or bus

— Guadalquivir

- - - Bicycle lane

Vision for the *The Eco-Traveller*

Seville, the capital of Andalusia, is directly located on the river Guadalquivir and is the economic centre of the area—in a strategic position between the Mediterranean Sea, the Atlantic Ocean, and the whole European continent. The area has a rich cultural heritage and a unique mixture of cultures, languages, and traditions. The investigation to detect circular dynamics starts from analysing the agriculture, the rural towns surrounding Seville, and the infrastructure. If the area is to continue its path of historical relevance in food production, the ecological impact derived from local activities needs to be considerably lowered and new sustainable approaches need to be developed, in particular preventing desertification (Junta de Andalucía 2008; Expósito, Berbel 2017).

The towns around Seville, partly due to the postponement of urbanisation processes since the 2008 economic crisis, are losing their young population and threatened by abandonment, particularly of historic centres. They can already rely on connectivity with Seville, but they have barely no connection with each other through public transport, and no sustainable transport of goods or lean mobility. There is not only a lack of infrastructural connectivity, but also of other aspects such as knowledge, economic initiatives, community projects, locally produced products, or cultural events. At the same time, local knowledge, traditions, and culture—important sources for a circular economy—are threatened. On the positive side, several projects and initiatives targeting the use of food by-products exist (Moore 2018; Alves de Castro et al. 2020; Pleguezuelo et al. 2018), direct production and distribution chains extend to Seville and its different transport hubs, while local initiatives and not least the tourism economy are rediscovering the cultural vocation of food production.

The scenario developed in order to foster circular systems in the towns and in linkages with Seville points at the river Guadalquivir as a new axis for the sustainable transport of people and goods on water, to be extended in the canal systems—the visible side of a new water regime with considerably less irrigation and adjustment of plants. This new transport axis links directly to the centre of Seville and to the harbour as an international hub. A boat system can become a tool for circular economy and cooperation. As part of a larger circular concept, the aim is to ensure better connection not only in terms of mobility but between people and enterprises: e.g. in support of ecological transformation, start-ups, education, training, new business models.

The concept of *The Eco-Traveller* proposes a travelling event in the form of performances and activities linked to a pavilion that travels from town to town, collects and distributes information, knowledge, products, and culture, and that enhances cooperation. The starting point of the travelling pavilion is the port of Seville—a key hub in the concept—from where it is transported by ship. When it is delivered to one of the new boat stops near the towns, its arrival is celebrated with a festival. Then the pavilion is set up in the centre of the town. Each of the towns organises a programme for the activities linked to the pavilion, derived from economic, social, and cultural characteristics, in particular concerning bio-economy. While some towns are already known for their agricultural activities and their products, others are noted for their cultural events and art

projects. *The Eco-Traveller* can connect these strengths and initiate the cultural change necessary for sustainable transition. In the pavilion, workshops, exhibitions, and events accelerate the exchange of information and bring entrepreneurs, experts, skilled workers, citizens, and tourists together. The pavilion takes the form of parasols and is therefore a flexible structure that can be adapted to different situations. After the period of activities, it travels to the next town and thus triggers a circular economy along the Guadalquivir. At the port of Seville, the home base of the pavilion, prototypes and products are sampled during the year and then presented all together at a fair event.

Analysis of the different situations and connectivity of towns

---

Poblado de Alfonso XIII

Puebla del Rio

La Algaba

Valdezorras

Torre de la Reina

Montequinto

Gerena

Huevar del Aljafarre

In order to verify the concept's impact, three different towns are chosen to draw scenarios. The spatial setting and adaptation of the pavilion in the town centre and the possible linkages to local innovative initiatives, projects, and enterprises are examined. In order to facilitate flexibility and adaptation, the pavilion structure has been designed for open as well as for closed spaces: hence, the concept is tested for a traditional main square (La Rinconada), a semi-closed courtyard (Torre de la Reina), and a wide main street (Huevar de Aljarafe).

The main aim of the pavilion is to create connection and exchange on an economic and social level. It is a manifesto to evolve a more sustainable and conscious way of using and cohabitating the towns and the land, responsibly sharing its huge resources and offering concrete tools to foster cooperation and innovation. This includes working with inherited knowledge and traditions for an eco-friendly production, as well as with digitalised production chains and information technology, facing local challenges and fighting climate change. Not only the food and agriculture sector, but other sectors can be involved in a bio-based circular economy and infrastructure measures. Several infrastructure projects that are already implemented not only in Seville but also in the towns, such as the bicycle lanes along the Guadalquivir, can be upscaled through regional cooperation.

The pavilion is also conceived to inspire people from Seville, guests, and visitors to contribute to creating new production chains and new culture, and then to disseminate the new image of the area and its circular achievements. Since ecological transition affects every aspect of life, the pavilion is also designed as a space of debate and knowledge exchange, to open up new horizons and provide a stage for discussion and cooperation. Throughout the whole investigation, the unique cultural richness of the area has been an exciting discovery, and the complex challenges an opportunity to approach new ways to face climate change, to limit ecological impact, and to become an active part of changes in the way we produce.

Bibliography:

Alves de Castro L., Lizi J. M., Leite das Chagas E., Aparecida de Carcalho R., Vanin F.M. (2020) "From orange juice by-product in the food industry to a functional ingredient: application in the circular economy". In: *Foods* 2020, 9(5), 593. DOI: http://doi.org/10.3390/foods9050593.

Expósito A., Berbel J. (2017) "Agricultural irrigation water use in a closed basin and the impacts on water productivity. The case of the Guadalquivir river basin (Southern Spain)". In: *Water* 2017, 9(2), 136. DOI: https://doi.org/10.3390/w9020136.

Junta de Andalucia (2008) *Rapport Technique Final du Projet DESERTNET II, Partenaire No. 7 Région Andalousie. Programme Interreg IIIB MEDOCC.* Available online at: http://www.juntadeandalucia.es/medioambiente/portal/landing-page-%C3%ADndice/-/asset_publisher/zX2ouZa4r1Rf/content/desernet-ii/20151 (01.06.2022).

Moore D. (2018) *Renewi working on 100% circular solution to reuse citrus peel.* Available online at: http://www.circularonline.co.uk/news/renewi-working-on-100-circular-solution-to-reuse-citrus-peel/ (01.06.2022).

Pleguezuelo C.R.R., Zuazo V. H. D., Martínez J. R. F., Peinado F. J. M., Martín F. M., Tejero I. F. G. (2018) "Organic olive farming in Andalusia, Spain. A review". In: *Agrononmy for Sustainable Development* 38, 20 (2018). DOI: http://doi.org/10.1007/s13593-018-0498-2.

1 Torre de la Reina pavilion location
2 Pavilion in the towns—prototype
3 Algaba pavilion location
4 Huévar del Alrajafe pavilion location
5 Arrival at the port of Seville
6 La Rinconada pavilion location

APPENDIX

Behind this Book

Jörg Schröder, architect and urban planner, Full professor and Chair for Territorial Design and Urban Planning of Leibniz University Hannover. Graduated from and assistant professor at Technische Universität München. His research focus is on urbanism and architecture for sustainable transition and territorial innovation, as well as on design research, particularly regarding new metropolitan and peripheral spatial constellations, emerging creative habitats, and circular dynamics. Recent R&D projects include: Rurbance (EU Alpine Space Programme), Regiobranding (BMBF), Dynamics of Periphery (DAAD), Creative Heritage (Volkswagen Foundation), Creative Food Cycles (EU Creative Europe Programme). schroeder@staedtebau.uni-hannover.de

Riccarda Cappeller M.Sc. M.A., University researcher and lecturer at the Chair for Territorial Design and Urban Planning of Leibniz University Hannover. Her research interest is in design modes for mixed urban spaces, conducting teaching and research activities on artistic approaches in urban design. Since 2015 she has been an architectural journalist, and since 2013 worked in collaboration with the collective Exyzt/Constructlab. MA in Visual Sociology at Goldsmiths University London 2017 and MSc in Architecture at Bauhaus Universität Weimar 2015, Universidad de Buenos Aires 2014, ETSAM, Politecnica Madrid 2012. cappeller@staedtebau.uni-hannover.de

Alissa Diesch, architect, university researcher and lecturer at the Chair for Territorial Design and Urban Planning of Leibniz University Hanover. Graduated from and teaching assignments at Technische Universität München (2016–2017). Researcher, lecturer and leader of the research group Hábitat Socio-Cultural at the Universidad La Gran Colombia, Bogotá (2015–18). Architect at Zwischenräume Architekten (2012–14). DAAD PhD research scholarship in Colombia 2017. Her research interests include participatory knowledge generation, postcolonial spaces, research-to-design concepts, rurban-rural relations and transformations. diesch@staedtebau.uni-hannover.de

Federica Scaffidi, architect, PhD, University researcher and lecturer at the Chair for Territorial Design and Urban Planning of Leibniz University Hannover. Visiting scholar at Polytechnic of Turin (2015–16), ETSAM of Madrid (2016), LUH (2017), and IUAV (2022). PhD and Doctor Europaeus from University of Palermo (2019). Her research is based on qualitative and quantitative methodologies and has addressed territorial development, social innovation and recycling, studying how creative cycles are driving new urban communities and social entrepreneurship models. scaffidi@staedtebau.uni-hannover.de

Anna Pape M.Sc., graduated in Architecture and Urban Design from Leibniz University Hanover. Research assistant and tutor at the Chair of Territorial Design and Urban Planning. In addition to her experience in several architecture and urban design offices in Hanover and Berlin, she cooperates for many projects as a collective with the artist Franz Betz devising projects in urban space and light installations. Recent publication: Urbane Optionsflächen, with Raumlabor Berlin. anna.pape@web.de appendix

Many thanks to all our fantastic students who contributed to the book: Lucie Paulina Bock, Maya Eberle, Vanessa Ehrich, Gülce Erincik, Kristina Gergert, Michel Grändorf, Juan Esteban Hernandez Cardona, Pia-Marie Hoff, Niccoló Huesmann, Jan Hüttmann, Pia Nicola Kampkötter, Leandra Leipold, Melanie Oeltjen, Tamás Oravecz-Deák, Malin Osterheider, Anna Pape, Max Passgang, Sarah Pens, Mara Piel, Karen Schäfer, Marius Schumann, Leonardo Stadler, Julia Theis, Rebekka Wandt, Lea von Wolfframsdorff.

New Bauhaus City: Master Territorial Design Studio directed by Jörg Schröder, Riccarda Cappeller, and Federica Scaffidi. Students: Aletta Bünte, Kristina Gergert, Pia-Marie Hoff, Niccoló Huesmann, Miriam Krüssel, Tamas Oravecz-Deák, Diana Ragimova, Karen Schäfer, Madita Schroeder, Marius Schumann, Cesia Vergara Torpoco, Jule Weiher, Faya Youssef.

Seaside: Master Territorial Design Studio directed by Jörg Schröder, Alissa Diesch, and Riccarda Cappeller. Students: Chen Daie, Maya Eberle, Dao Le, Andrea Marcos Pelaez, Alba Marín Pérez, Christina Mauersberg, Nolwenn Maurice, Malin Osterheider, Max Passgang, Soleia Pierre, Leonardo Stadler, Lisa-Marie Tegt, Rebecca Wehling, Laura Wirbel.

Mountains: Master Territorial Design Studio directed by Jörg Schröder, Alissa Diesch, and Federica Scaffidi. Students: Gabriel Cameron, Ricco Frank, Angela Gaini, Michel Grändorf, Anna Kozachkova, Nadine Kristandt, Ajda Lukman, Emma Römer, Pia Schulenberg, Vanessa Schwarzkopf, Karina Tews, Rebekka Wandt, Nicolas Witt, Hans von Witzendorff.

Medways: Circular Territories: Master Territorial Design Seminar directed by Jörg Schröder, Riccarda Cappeller, Alissa Diesch, and Federica Scaffidi. Students: Vanessa Ehrich, Gülce Erincik, Juan Esteban Hernandez Cardona, Niccoló Huesmann, Jan Hüttmann, Melanie Oeltjen, Tamás Oravecz-Deák, Sarah Pens.

Thesis projects in the chapters New Systems, New Processes, and Transformation, supervised by Jörg Schröder, Riccarda Cappeller, Alissa Diesch, and Federica Scaffidi: Lucie Paulina Bock, Pia Nicola Kampkötter, Leandra Leipold, Mara Piel, Julia Theis, Rebekka Wandt, Lea von Wolfframsdorff; as well as "Pacman" by Anna Pape and Julia Theis as Master Studio project. Special thanks to Prof. Dr. Dr. Margitta Buchert as second examiner of most of the thesis projects at the Chair.

Instagram: **@territorialdesign**

More Books

Schröder J., Scaffidi F., eds. (2020) Palermo Open City. ISBN 978-3-946296-32-4.

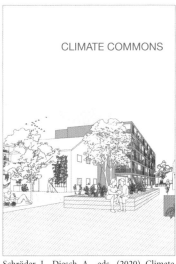

Schröder J., Diesch A., eds. (2020) Climate Commons. ISBN 978-3-946296-31-7.

Schröder J., Cappeller R., eds. (2020) Cosmopolitan Habitat: Urban Narratives. ISBN 978-3-946296-34-8.

Schröder J., Cappeller R., eds. (2021) Hangar Explorations. The RAW Area in Halle/Saale. ISBN 978-3-946296-38-6.

MOUNTAINS

Schröder J., Diesch A., eds. (2021) Mountains. New Habitat Explorations. ISBN 978-3-946296-38-6.

LAKESHORE

Schröder J., Cappeller R., eds. (2021) Lakeshore: Cosmopolitan Habitat. ISBN 978-3-946296-36-2.

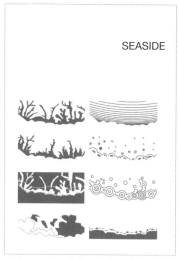

SEASIDE

Schröder J., Diesch A., eds. (2022) Seaside. A Creative Platform for Coast Territories. ISBN 978-3-946296-41-6.

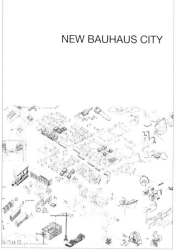

NEW BAUHAUS CITY

Schröder J., Cappeller R., eds. (2021) New Bauhaus City. Rediscovering territories outside of metropolis. ISBN 978-3-946296-39-3.

Circular Design
Towards Regenerative Territories
by Jörg Schröder, Riccarda Cappeller, Alissa Diesch, and Federica Scaffidi

Copy-editing: Melissa Larner
Design and Setting: Anna Pape
Cover: Graphic by Anna Pape
Chapter covers: Graphic by Anna Pape based on Google Maps

Printed in the European Union

Bibliographic information published by the Deutsche Nationalbibliothek:
The Deutsche Nationalbibliothek lists this publication in the Deutsche
Nationalbibliografie; detailed bibliographic data are available on the internet at
http://dnb.d-nb.de

jovis Verlag GmbH
Lützowstraße 33
10785 Berlin

www.jovis.de

jovis books are available worldwide in selected bookstores. Please contact your nearest
bookseller or visit www.jovis.de for information concerning your local distribution.

ISBN 978-3-86859-745-5 (Softcover)
ISBN 978-3-86859-836-0 (PDF)